planet burnout

how to decrease overwhelm + live a more sustainable life

THE SKILL COLLECTIVE

First published in 2021 by The Skill Collective.

Copyright ©The Skill Collective 2021.
Developed by Joyce Chong.
The moral rights of the author have been asserted.

All rights reserved. No part of this publication may be reproduced, stored in a retrieval system, or transmitted in any form or by any means, electronic, mechanical, photocopying, recording or otherwise without the prior permission in writing by the publisher. This book is sold subject to the condition that it shall not be resold, lent, hired out or otherwise circulated without the expressed prior consent of the publisher.

Every reasonable effort has been made to trace the copyright holders of material in this book. Any errors or omissions should be notified in writing to the publisher, who will endeavour to rectify the situations for any reprints and future editions.

Disclaimer
The information contained within this book, whilst based on scientific literature, is intended to be general in nature and does not negate personal responsibility on the part of the reader for their own health and safety. It is recommended that the reader seeks individually tailored advice from a qualified healthcare professional. The publishers and their respective employees, and authors, are not liable for injuries or damage occasioned to any person as a result of reading or following the information contained within this book.

Planet Burnout
ISBN: 978-0-6453375-0-1 in paperback print format

1 2 3 4 5 6 7 8 9 10

The Skill Collective
www.TheSkillCollective.com

To those
living on Planet Burnout,
we dedicate this book to helping
you build a more sustainable
and enjoyable life.

May you thrive.

CONTENTS

A TALE OF TWO PLANETS — 8

Are you living on Planet Burnout? — 10
Rogue Nations — 12

UNDERSTANDING PLANET BURNOUT — 14

At the Core of Burnout — 16
Piecing together the Layers of your Burnout — 26

REVITALISING PLANET BURNOUT

1. IDENTITY — 35

People-pleasing — 36
Type A personality — 37
Imposter syndrome — 38
Perfectionism — 45
Is busy your identity? — 50
The identity shift — 52

2. MINDSET — 55

Mindset 101: The basics — 56
Unhelpful thinking styles in burnout — 58
Social comparison — 64
Self-compassion — 66
Fixed vs growth mindset — 70
Flip the script — 72

3. ACTIONS — 84

Lifestyle + burnout	86
Why sleep matters	90
Exercise	94
Diet	94
Lifestyle vices	95
Slow down	96
Mindfulness + burnout	100
Managing yourself	104
Self-sabotaging behaviours	106
Just say no	111
Streamline	116
Managing time + energy	124
Taking action	136

4. OUTCOMES — 140

5. BEHAVIOUR CHANGE — 142

The right mindset for change	143
Making changes stick	144
Tracking your progress	146

REFERENCES — 148

NOTES — 153

A TALE OF

Once upon a time there existed two planets - Planet Burnout and Planet Engagement.

Life on Planet Burnout is challenging, where:

- You feel drained and exhausted. Weekends are used to catch up, and leaveism (using personal time to catch up on work) is a familiar concept.
- You detach from work, caring less about the impact and about the work itself.
- You feel less and less effective.

On Planet Burnout there are unhelpful mindset and thinking traps that constantly push you to do more. Poor lifestyle choices mean self-care is regularly scrimped on, leaving you without rest and recuperation.

In short, life on Planet Burnout involves being constantly on the go, but getting nowhere and feeling overwhelmed by it all.

TWO PLANETS

Is there an alternative to life on Planet Burnout? Why yes! Let's look at life on Planet Engagement where:

- Your mindset helps you stay energised and engaged. It helps you stay motivated to work in a sustainable manner to achieve your goals, rather than going at a million miles an hour and feeling overwhelmed.

- You recognise the importance of self-care to help you stay in peak condition. You dedicate time to replenish and rejuvenate after an intense period of activity.

- You live life at a sustainable pace, setting appropriate boundaries so you manage your workload and are able to maintain vigour and dedication.

- You're able to be in the moment, rather than living life ruminating about past events or worrying about the future.

- You focus on things that really matter, rather than living a life of clutter. You feel fulfilled.

ARE YOU LIVING ON
PLANET BURNOUT?

Are you a living on Planet Burnout? Whilst burnout is traditionally seen as consisting of emotional exhaustion, detachment from work, and reduced effectiveness, research from the Black Dog Institute indicates additional features of burnout, including:

- Anxiety or stress
- Irritability and anger
- Low mood/depression
- Physical ailments such as headaches, pains, low libido
- Social withdrawal
- Diminished motivation or passion
- Problematic sleep
- Inability to concentrate, forgetfulness, brain fog

Furthermore, burnout isn't seen as exclusively work-related. Let's take a closer look at how experiences of burnout may vary for different individuals.

Emily

Emily is juggling a part time job with a young family. Prior to having children, she valued being in control and excelling at anything she attempted.

However, she now finds herself overwhelmed as she tries to stay on top of everything. Emily finds herself scrimping on sleep to keep up, but feels like it's never good enough.

Will

Will is well-established in his career, holds an executive position at work, and is seen as Mr Fix-It and a mentor to many as well. He feels overwhelmed trying to live up to his reputation, and spends an inordinate amount of time keeping up his knowledge of the field.

The pressure Will places on himself means he is burning out. His focus on work also means that he neglects other areas, and it is now causing problems in his personal life.

Ty

Ty's burnout stems from wanting to please people and avoid conflict. Ty finds it hard to say no to others, takes on too much, and ends up neglecting other responsibilities.

Ali

Ali is a conscientious student, who spends every waking moment studying. However, the pressure he places on himself leads him to feel overwhelmed and he procrastinates as a result.

Predictably, burnout creeps in at the end of semester and Ali barely has enough fuel in the tank to get through exams. He often feels like a failure.

Heni

Heni is in the early stages of her career and in a hurry to prove herself and make a good impression at work.

She takes every opportunity that comes her way and finds it hard to say no to more work. Long hours at work are the norm, leaving her little time for self-care. To unwind, Heni drinks alcohol and stays up late to enjoy some down time, often to the detriment of the next day at work.

COMPASSION FATIGUE + VICARIOUS TRAUMA

Compassion fatigue is a type of burnout affecting individuals caring for those exposed to emotional or physical pain.

Compassion fatigue is often found in health workers and those in roles involving exposure to distressing or upsetting content (e.g. emergency services, legal, crisis support). Left unchecked, it can lead to a loss of passion for the role and prematurely leaving an otherwise fulfilling career.

Repeated exposure to others' trauma can also lead to the development of vicarious trauma including a shift in your world views as well as the experiencing of trauma symptoms.

ROGUE NATIONS
when burnout goes rogue

When burnout goes unchecked it can easily turn into mental health disorders such as anxiety and depression. Read on to learn more about why it's important to stop burnout in its tracks before it goes rogue.

ANXIETY

Anxiety can lead to burnout by predisposing you to interpret situations as threatening, which in turn increases your stress levels. This can drive you to work harder in order to eliminate the threat. For example, if you worry about your performance and want to prove your worth, you may work excessive hours or take on extra projects.

However, constantly pushing yourself too hard can lead you to live under a never-ending state of anxiety or heightened stress, and burnout follows.

NOT JUST PSYCHOLOGICAL...

Burnout doesn't just affect you psychologically. It can have real consequences for your physical health and lifestyle. Indeed, burnout is linked to insomnia, high blood pressure, heart disease, and an impacted immune system.

The good news is that taking care of your physical health through exercise, nutrition, and sleep can lessen the impact of burnout.

ALCOHOL + DRUG USE

Burnout can be tiring emotionally and also physically - you feel both overwhelmed and exhausted.

When this is your daily grind, it's easy to see why drugs and alcohol become appealing as a temporary relief from your overwhelm.

However, when how you unwind affects your ability to function the next day, or it stops you from meeting your responsibilities, then perhaps it's less of a solution to your woes and is now part of the burnout problem.

BURNOUT OR DEPRESSION

Burnout can feel similar to depression when you're experiencing emotional exhaustion, detaching from your work, and feeling like you're falling behind.

However, whilst burnout is specific to work, depression cuts across many areas of your life, affecting friendships and relationships, and limiting your quality of life. So if you find this to be the case, feel down most of the time, lack enjoyment and motivation, and aren't as active anymore, then depression may be setting in.

REACH OUT

If you notice that your burnout is going rogue, please get in touch with a mental health professional to see how they can help.

Reducing burnout isn't just about learning to manage your schedule better and engaging in more self-care. To live more sustainably, consider the many layers of burnout.

You see, burnout isn't purely a work issue even though workload, organisational culture, and job design are contributing factors. From an individual perspective, burnout reflects identity, mindset, and actions that lead to unhelpful outcomes.

Here we shine a light on the layers of *your* burnout. From this, you can build skills that make meaningful changes to reduce burnout and live more sustainably.

AT THE CORE OF BURNOUT

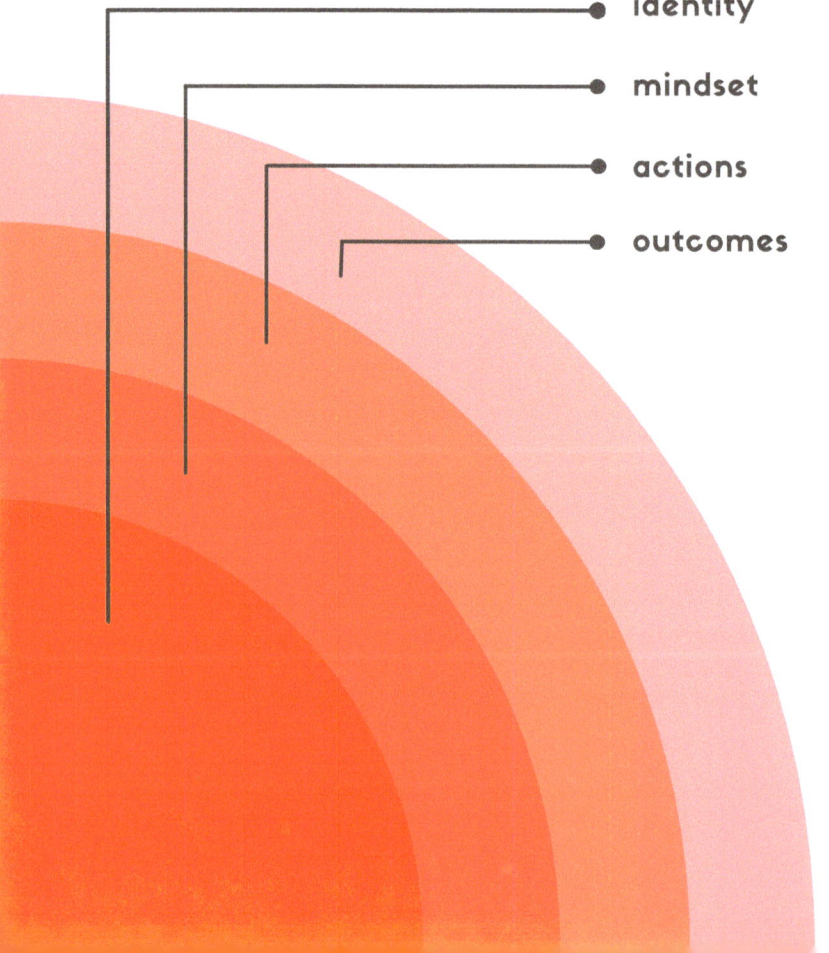

- identity
- mindset
- actions
- outcomes

identity

Your identity - or how you see yourself - can often lead you to take on too much and down the path to burnout.

- Perhaps you pride yourself on being capable, and that leads you to pour 110% into everything that you do.
- Maybe you like to be liked, and therefore shy away from setting boundaries and end up taking on more than you can handle.
- Or, perhaps you believe that achievements are only worthy if they're borne of great suffering. That is, you see burnout as a badge of honour, and testament to your efforts and abilities.

mindset

From identity comes mindset, which has many layers to it, including:

- Expectations that stem from your identity ("I must be agreeable in order for others to like me", "I must be knowledgeable") or of upcoming events ("My speech must be flawless else they'll see I'm incompetent").
- Beliefs and interpretations ("I did a terrible job!").
- Unhelpful thinking styles (for example, catastrophising, mind reading) that affect judgements and evaluations ("I only did well because they felt sorry for me!").

actions

A natural outcome of thinking is doing, and actions that lead to burnout include:

- Not setting boundaries to only take on what you can manage.
- Procrastinating (initially) due to overwhelm, which turns today's problem into a greater 'tomorrow problem'.
- Being 'extra', in that you must go beyond what is expected of you in order to prove yourself.

outcomes

When it feels like you're juggling so many things, it's not surprising that outcomes include stress, overwhelm, and burnout.

at the core of burnout

identity
who are you?

Understanding who you are, how you see yourself, and how you'd like others to see you is vital to understanding why burnout occurs. It shapes your mindset and influences your actions.

However, it can be tricky - sometimes even downright confronting - for some to articulate who they are. If this is the case, try these prompts to help reflect on how you view yourself:

- How would you describe yourself in five phrases?

- It's your 100th birthday and the important people in your life have gathered to celebrate you. What would you like to be remembered for?

- What is the worst thing that someone could think about you?

common identity themes in burnout

When it comes to burnout and identity, there are common themes that emerge. Those outlined below are by no means an exhaustive list, but a good starting point to help you dig deeper into uncovering how your identity fuels your burnout.

perfectionism

Perfectionism is considered to be a predisposing factor for burnout because of a tendency towards self-criticism, a focus on achieving excellence, and the conscientiousness and diligence often linked to perfectionism.

Other commonly seen characteristics of perfectionism include concern over mistakes, wanting to be faultless, and doubts over actions.

Unrealistic standards are also a feature of perfectionism.

Type A personality

Individuals with Type A personalities are driven to achieve, seek to gain control over situations, are competitive, and focused on deadlines. They push themselves hard to meet their goals, and are prime for burnout.

imposter syndrome

Imposter syndrome, or feeling like a fraud, occurs when you aren't able to internalise your objective successes.

Worrying about being found out can lead to excessive efforts in order to 'hide' perceived shortcomings.

people-pleasing + sensitivity to criticism

Needing to be liked by others and being sensitive to criticism predispose an individual's mood to fluctuate according to the approval (or disapproval) of others.

This can lead to poor boundary setting and a focus on behaving in ways that meet others' approval, even if it leads to burnout.

A common factor across these themes is that of **self-esteem**, specifically self-esteem linked to an outcome – be it the achievement of a task, or the approval of others – these essentially boil down to being 'good enough'.

If any of these sound familiar stay tuned as we dive deeper into these topics throughout Planet Burnout.

at the core of burnout

what role does mindset play in burnout?

Mindset shapes burnout in many different ways: expectations, fixed mindsets, beliefs and interpretations, and unhelpful thinking styles. In this section we take a closer look at the many parts of mindset and their impact on burnout.

THE HAPPINESS OF YOUR LIFE DEPENDS ON THE QUALITY OF YOUR THOUGHTS

Marcus Aurelius

expectations

Expectations can really lead us down the path to burnout in how we see ourselves, others, and the world. It's easy to spot these expectations that push us to do more - there is normally a 'should' or 'must' in play. For instance:

- "I should be able to cope with anything thrown at me."
- "I must not rock the boat otherwise people will be angry."
- "They expect us to be contactable at all times, it's just the norm at our workplace."
- "In order for an achievement to be worthwhile I must suffer in the process of attaining it."
- "I should say yes to all work in order to prove myself."

According to Carol Dweck, a fixed mindset occurs when you believe ability and intelligence are fixed. Holding this frame of mind means that when either of these are threatened (for example facing challenges or setbacks), it can lead to excessive preparation or efforts in order to avoid failure.

fixed vs growth mindset

beliefs + interpretations

Beliefs you hold, and interpretations you make, about yourself and of events, have the power to influence what actions you take and, in turn, lead you to burnout.

These may include negative beliefs you hold about your abilities, about the complexity of a task, and about the outcome. These all influence your motivation and the actions you take.

Unhelpful thinking styles in burnout refer to distorted patterns of thinking that have a negative effect on your mood. These can lead to an inflated sense of threat and contribute to heightened stress and burnout.

Common unhelpful thinking styles observed in burnout include: all or nothing thinking, 'shoulds' and 'musts', personalisation, catastrophising, and mind reading. These are discussed in greater detail later on in Planet Burnout.

unhelpful thinking styles

at the core of burnout

actions

In response to your mindset, and particularly those beliefs and interpretations that you hold in response to events, the actions you take can result in burnout:

- You do nothing, and let the situation continue as is. However, nothing changes if nothing changes - the triggers for burnout will still be there and you have addressed neither the cause nor the outcomes.

- You avoid things, likely due to experiencing negative emotions. Procrastination is a prime example of avoidance. The difficulty with avoidance is that the problem doesn't go away, and may even worsen when you eventually return to it and cause greater overwhelm.

- You attack things head on to get the job done. However, you approach it in a manner or intensity that leads you to feel overworked and burnt out.

at the core of burnout

outcomes

The actions that you take in response to your identity and mindset can have a negative impact on your physical and psychological health.

Burnout is just one of the consequences, and when it is left untreated it can 'go rogue' and lead to serious mental health issues (refer to the earlier section Rogue Nations: when burnout goes rogue).

Piecing together THE LAYERS OF YOUR BURNOUT
Case studies

Before we move on to revitalising Planet Burnout, let's drill down to understand what's at the core of *your* burnout. Take a closer look at Planet Burnout's inhabitants and how identity, mindset, actions, and outcomes make up the layers of their burnout. Follow this up with your own reflections.

 Emily

Identity Perfectionistic, Type A personality style. Wants to be seen as being in control.

Mindset Difficulties adjusting to new role in life, and juggling the various components of it. Holds herself up to ideals that are not realistic given her various commitments.

Actions Scrimps on self-care in order to squeeze everything into the day.

Outcomes Feels inadequate and out of control, as well as exhausted.

 Ali

Identity Perfectionistic, Type A personality style.

Mindset Expects to dedicate himself entirely to studies during the semester, and any other activities are seen as a waste of productive time. Reactive to signs of failure.

Actions Procrastinates due to stress then studies intensely to meet deadlines. Rarely engages in self-care.

Outcomes Frazzled and burnt-out, often experiencing this prior to exams.

Ty

Identity People-pleasing and conflict-avoidant.

Mindset Expects others to react negatively and is hypervigilant for signs of others' displeasure or rejection. Interprets comments as a sign of criticism.

Actions Finds it hard to say no and ends up taking on and prioritising others' requests (to his own detriment). Goes above and beyond when doing tasks for others.

Outcomes Feels overwhelmed, and falls behind on own workload. At times feels underappreciated and even used by others.

Will

Identity Imposter syndrome.

Mindset Worries about others 'finding out' that he is not as good as they expect him to be. Hypervigilant to signs of criticism. Discounts praise.

Actions Extremely work-focused and spends a lot of time staying abreast of knowledge in his field. Neglects other areas of his life.

Outcomes Rarely feels adequate. Feels overwhelmed, exhausted, and his focus on work is affecting his physical health and relationships.

Heni

Identity Type A personality style, perfectionistic.

Mindset Sees every opportunity as a chance to prove herself. Holds high expectations of herself in order to fit in to a high-performance work culture where long hours are the norm.

Actions Neglects self-care, engages in unhelpful coping behaviours (using alcohol, scrimps on sleep).

Outcomes Exhausted due to long work hours and insufficient self-care. Self-esteem rises and falls with feedback at work. Friendships and relationships suffer due to Heni's hyperfocus on work.

your turn...
Use the next couple of pages to map out the layers of your burnout.

IDENTITY

How does your identity contribute to your burnout? Reflect on the following:

- What would you like others to remember you for?
- What is the worst thing that someone can think about you?

MINDSET

- How does your identity bias your focus in everyday life? (For example, if you pride yourself on being capable you may expect yourself to grasp things easily and be more likely to tune in to signs of poor performance.)
- What unhelpful interpretations and unhelpful thinking styles do you notice on a regular basis that leads to your burnout?

ACTIONS

What do you do (or avoid doing) that lead you to feel overwhelmed? Consider:

- Tasks and activities you commit to because they are in line with your identity and how you view yourself.
- Actions you take because of your interpretations and unhelpful thinking styles, that lead you down the path to burnout.

OUTCOMES

Given all that you take on, how are you left feeling?

what's at the **core** of your **burnout**?

REVITALISING PLANET BURNOUT

Now that you understand what is at the core of your burnout, let's look to revitalising your wellbeing. So what does it take to recover from burnout and move towards resilience?

Bouncing back from burnout will need more than just taking a few weeks off. Given the many layers of your burnout, it will take a multifaceted approach to bring about change.

you've got to nourish to flourish

In this section of Planet Burnout we look at a template for making shifts in identity, mindset, and actions. We'll also take a closer look at how to make these changes sustainable.

By learning how to sustain these changes in the longer term, you become more resilient and are better able to prevent burnout in the future.

choosing to change

What will you change to bounce back from burnout?

When it comes to bouncing back from burnout, it's helpful to focus on making changes that are primarily within your locus of control.

- What is within your circle of control? These relate to problems involving your own actions. Your impact will be greatest here.
- What is within your circle of influence? You can try to change these, but recognise that you have indirect control over outcomes.
- What is within your circle of concern? Whilst you may feel passionate about these, you likely have little influence over outcomes.

1. Shift underlying **identity** issues that drive you closer to burnout. Perfectionism, people-pleasing, and imposter syndrome are all part of this. Practise self-compassion to shift demands you make of yourself.

2. Shift your unhelpful **mindset** (expectations, beliefs, and thinking styles) in order to improve resilience and reduce distress.

3. Take **action** on burnout by doing things differently. This may include approaching rather than avoiding a task, managing time and energy better, as well as practising self-care.

4. Evaluate **outcomes** of the shifts you've made to identity, mindset, and actions.

5. Understand how to remain motivated and stay on track for sustainable **behaviour change** when it comes to burnout.

a template for change

TO BE YOURSELF
IN A WORLD THAT IS
CONSTANTLY TRYING
TO MAKE YOU
SOMETHING ELSE
IS THE **GREATEST**
ACCOMPLISHMENT

Ralph Waldo Emerson

1

IDENTITY

Identity. It's at the core of our burnout - how we see ourselves drives our mindset, actions, and outcomes.

In this section we explore how to shift unhelpful aspects of your identity in order to live a more sustainable life.

Of particular note, due to the impact of perfectionism and imposter syndrome on burnout, we dive deeper into these.

PEOPLE-PLEASING

If your burnout is due to people-pleasing, perhaps it's time to reflect on how well this is serving you. Here are some ways to re-set.

IT'S A TWO-WAY STREET

Prioritising the needs and preferences of others over your own leads to one-sided friendships. Resentment can then build up to the point where you feel taken advantage of, feel unimportant, or even invisible.

It's helpful to reflect on the impact of this dynamic on your self-esteem, and how it adds to your burnout.

YOUR OPINION MATTERS

Perhaps you fear conflict and view being assertive as being on par with being aggressive. Maybe this has led you to lose sight of your opinions, and you feel voiceless.

So what would you do if the opinion of others didn't matter? What would you speak up about? What injustices would get you fired up?

TAKING RESPONSIBILITY

You may wish to avoid causing others hurt (and being the bad guy!), but bear in mind that others are also responsible for their own feelings.

CONTROL CENTRE

When your life revolves around control and predictability, coping with unexpected changes can cause significant overwhelm.

What difference would it make to your burnout if you were able to go with the flow? Perhaps it's time to loosen the reins of control.

NOT EVERYTHING IS A COMPETITION

Striving for achievement is a hallmark of Type A personalities, but not everything is a competition. Unhelpful comparisons with others can lead you to push harder to outdo them, but is this healthy or does it take you closer to burnout?

SLOW DOWN

Why the rush? There will always be places to get to, and tasks to complete. If you continue to go at this pace, burnout is inevitable. Focus instead on working at a more sustainable pace.

TYPE A PERSONALITY

With their concern over deadlines and a focus on achievement and competitiveness, what can Type A personalities do to help burnout?

IMPOSTER SYNDROME

*when you're falling apart
because you feel like a fraud*

WHAT IS IMPOSTER SYNDROME?

Imposter syndrome occurs when you believe yourself to be undeserving of your achievements, and instead feel inadequate. Rather, successes are believed to result from luck or somehow pulling the wool over someone's eyes. You may even worry you'll be found out to be a fraud.

It's estimated that imposter syndrome has been experienced by around 70% of people. Whilst some believe imposter syndrome reflects stable personality traits, it may be triggered by situations such as:

- 'Stepping up' a level, such as gaining a promotion at work.

- Gaining a qualification, or becoming 'fully-fledged' in your profession following the completion of a traineeship.

- Others looking up to you and asking you for your thoughts and opinions, such as when you're in a position of seniority.

Do you have imposter syndrome?

It's quite easy to detect if you have imposter syndrome. Ask yourself:
- Do you think that someone will find you out?
- Do you think that you got to where you are in life through sheer luck?
- Is it hard for you to acknowledge your achievements? Do you explain them away as being due to luck or the task being easy?

Is imposter syndrome the same for everyone?

Interestingly, imposter syndrome does not look the same for everyone. Psychologist Valerie Young, in her book 'The Secret Thoughts of Successful Women', outlined five types of imposter syndrome depending on their triggers:

The 'Perfectionist' has unrelenting standards, and imposter syndrome is triggered when there is deviation (however small) from the attainment of these standards.

The 'Expert' strives to know everything in the field, thus feeling uncertain can trigger imposter syndrome.

The 'Soloist' is solitary in their approach to attaining goals, and asking for help triggers a sense of inadequacy and failure.

The 'Natural Genius' is used to achieving success easily and effortlessly, and when something requires effort it's seen as a sign of failure.

The 'Superhero' thrives on excelling in the various areas of their life. Falling short in any of these areas can trigger feelings of inadequacy.

Which imposter syndrome type do you most identify with?

How does imposter syndrome influence your actions?

How is imposter syndrome linked to burnout?

Looking over the different types of imposter syndrome, it's easy to see how it leads to burnout. For example:

- The 'Perfectionist' holds high standards that are unrealistic, unrelenting, and often unattainable. Any deviation, however small, may be seen as failure. It's this and a fear of failure that leads to excessive workloads, thus paving the way to burnout.

- No one can ever know absolutely everything about a topic. However, the 'Expert' feels pressured to do so, and can exhaustively search all available information before making a decision for fear of looking foolish. Unfortunately, needing to know everything before taking action can result in analysis paralysis. Whilst a decision is delayed, time pressure builds up and stress and burnout ensue.

- That the 'Soloist' feels the need to achieve based solely on their efforts, in reality many modern day goals - particularly in the workplace - require the involvement of other people, knowledge, and skills. This may lead the 'Soloist' to spend a lot of time 'catching up' on background knowledge for an unfamiliar topic prior to even starting the actual task at hand. Certainly, it would take less time (and cause less stress) to consult with someone more knowledgeable in the field.

- The 'Natural Genius' may feel like failures when faced with a challenging task, and may either attack it or 'check out' altogether due to a sense of inadequacy. Feeling less than capable can lead to subjective feelings of not coping (reduced efficacy), which can result in burnout.

- The 'Superhero' cannot realistically excel in all areas of life given time constraints. Yet attempting to achieve these lofty goals inflates time and energy commitments - a surefire recipe for burnout.

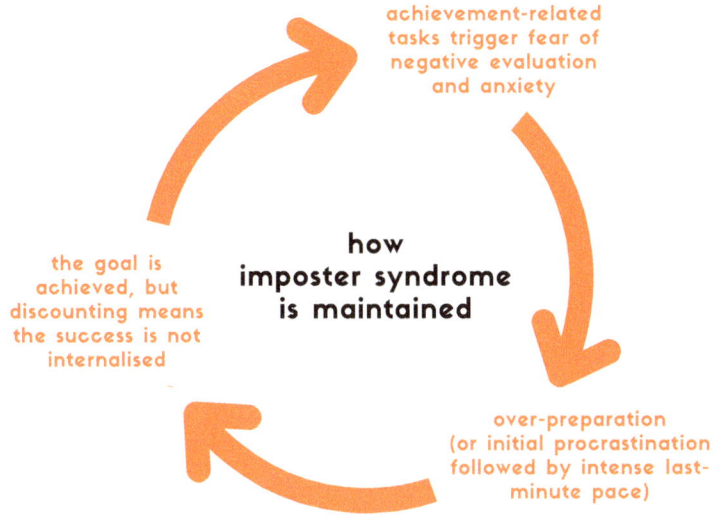

The imposter cycle

Imposter syndrome is maintained via the imposter cycle in which achievement-related tasks trigger anxiety and a fear of negative evaluation.

When this happens, excessive preparation is likely to occur, perhaps even following initial procrastination (due to the task triggering anxiety or fear).

Unfortunately, successes can easily be discounted ("They were being nice!", "I only did well as I over-prepared!") rather than acknowledged as a personal achievement. The link between discounting and burnout is covered in more detail in the Mindset section of this workbook.

Perfectionism. It's often viewed positively – it gets the job done, and gets it done well. Indeed, many view it beneficial to have a perfectionist on their team when it comes to projects. Yet perfectionism is not all sunshine and rainbows.

Healthy or adaptive perfectionism occurs when you set high and realistic goals and work towards them. Achievement yields satisfaction, but mistakes are tolerated in healthy perfectionism and seen as learning opportunities. As part of this, self-esteem remains largely robust and intact.

Perfectionism also has an unhealthy or maladaptive side. This happens when there is the relentless pursuit of unrealistic goals, your self-worth is based on achieving these goals, and striving for these goals comes at a significant negative cost to you.

It's easy to see how unhealthy perfectionism leads you to overwhelm and burnout. Indeed, perfectionism has been identified as a key contributing factor to burnout. In this section we take a closer look at the grip of unhealthy perfectionism.

PERFECTIONISM

Feeling under the pump as perfectionism inflates the amount of time spent on tasks.

Feeling inadequate.

the price of your
PERFECTIONISM

Constant stress + anxiety.

Working endlessly until it feels 'just right'.

the price of your PERFECTIONISM

Failing to reach your unrelenting standards.

Procrastinating starting a task because you're afraid it won't be good enough.

Delaying making a decision in case you choose the incorrect one.

Focusing on failures rather than successes.

the price of
PERFECTIONISM

Perfectionism comes in different forms, affecting people in different ways at different points in their lives. Let's take a closer look at some ways in which perfectionism is experienced.

Ali

Ali the student has struggled since making the jump from high school to university. In school his unrelenting standards helped him excel in his studies. At university, however, he finds he is unable to stay on top of his study load and can't meet his unrelenting standards. Perfectionism affects Ali in the following ways:

- He places his life on hold during semester as he spends every waking hour studying. When he doesn't feel productive, he believes he is lazy.

- Mood and self-worth suffer as these are closely linked to marks. Anything less than a High Distinction is seen by Ali as failure.

- Ali feels lonely and disconnected from friends but study comes first.

- With all the pressure Ali places on himself he ends up procrastinating, which reinforces his view of himself as lazy. Ali feels overwhelmed and exhausted, yet ineffective.

Will

Will has excelled in all areas of his life - academically, physically, and also socially. Perfectionism has helped him climb to the top of his organisation, but it is now causing him burnout.

- Will's drive and energy meant he was able to work long hours to get to the top of his organisation. He is seen to be a subject matter expert. Others look to him as Mr Fix-It, and seek his wisdom and leadership on projects.

- On the inside though, Will struggles to live up to his Mr Fix-It reputation. He feels that he is only as good as the problems he solves, and spends an excessive amount of time outside of work reading up on his field so he is prepared for any questions he may be asked. He often feels like an imposter waiting to be found out.

- The time spent focusing on work means he neglects his family. He also comfort eats to distract himself from his feelings. His solution to this is to prove himself by doing more.

 ## Emily

Emily juggles her part time job with a young family. She has always excelled at everything she attempts, and is used to having every aspect of her life under control. Emily's perfectionism affects her such that:

- In spite of recognising that she has taken on the additional role of parenting, Emily interprets her stress at the 'struggle of the juggle' as a sign that she is not in control.

- She compares herself to her friends, to colleagues, even to strangers on social media who seem to have it all and be in control. She compares her output at work to those working full-time. She compares the time she spends with her children to full-time parents. And she compares what she does for her children - meals that she makes, parties that she throws - to what she sees on social media and feels inadequate.

- In an attempt to meet the goals she sets for herself in the various areas of her life, she stays up late. The down side is that she is exhausted, and her wellbeing and the quality of her interactions with her family are affected. Emily's self-esteem is thus further eroded, and she feels that nothing she does is good enough.

What is the price of your perfectionism?

What impact has perfectionism had on your work and personal life? What about your quality of life?

How does perfectionism affect your mood and self-esteem?

> *People are often so busy living that they never stop to wonder why.*
> — TERRY PRATCHETT

Has being busy become your identity? Those with Type A personality styles might agree with this as they power through never-ending To Do lists, meetings, and other commitments. Being busy is equated with being productive, achieving, and succeeding. But what is the cost of wearing busyness as a badge of honour and constantly rushing against the clock? Is it time to slow down?

Those who value being busy find slowing down particularly challenging, and will often set goal-based leisure activities. Thus, it is not about going for a walk in the park, but instead becomes about walking a certain distance in a certain amount of time. Playing a team sport to relax and connect with others becomes about match statistics. Doing nothing is often a foreign concept because it is tricky to quantify success in doing nothing.

And yet, slowing down has never been more important in this busy culture. Time to reflect, restore, and rejuvenate helps you to connect with yourself, with others, and with your environment. It gives you time to appreciate what you cherish and to focus on what's important. These are all helpful in managing burnout, and tips to help you to slow down are covered in the Action section of this workbook.

The IDENTITY SHIFT

Making an identity shift can be confronting. *Really* confronting. You've lived your entire life thus far seeing yourself a particular way, and now you're considering turning it on its head. But fear not. You're not looking to pivot by 180 degrees. All you're looking to do is to shift slightly so that your life can be more sustainable than this existence you lead on Planet Burnout.

In the earlier section on Understanding Planet Burnout we looked at how you would describe yourself and what you would like to be remembered for. In this section, reflect on the following:

- Imagine that the world is ending in 24hrs. How would you choose to spend your time? What really matters to you?

- Next, what is 'nice to have' but not essential to the bigger picture. What is noise that just distracts?

- Now... how do you spend your time? On things that are important to you and form part of your identity, or on non-essentials and distractions?

Hopefully this exercise helps crystallise what matters to you, and what should form the core of your identity. If you find that you still lack clarity around your identity and your values, consider taking the Values in Action Strengths Survey.

 **Emily**

 **Will**

Always-in-control Emily expects herself to be perfect in the various roles in her life, and aiming for this leads to burnout.

The main identity shift for Emily to make is to recognise which role is the priority for her, and to reflect on whether the manner in which she spends her time reflects this priority.

Acceptance will be an important part of Emily's identity shift. Recognising that she has a limited number of hours in a day means she is making choices to spend time on what is important to her.

Perfectionism and imposter syndrome keep Will stuck on Planet Burnout as he tries to live up to his Mr Fix-It reputation.

The main identity shift for Will to make is to recognise that being a leader and a mentor isn't about having all of the answers, but instead to encourage and inspire others to strive to constantly learn. Shifting away from living up to an idealised version of himself, to one that shows vulnerability and a willingness to lead, frees Will from needing to always have the answers.

What identity shifts will help you make the shift away from burnout?

Hopefully this exercise helps identify what matters to you, and what should form the core of your identity. If you find that you still lack clarity around your identity and values, consider completing the Values in Action Strengths Survey.

THE IDENTITY SHIFT

THE **GREATEST WEAPON** AGAINST STRESS IS OUR ABILITY TO **CHOOSE** ONE THOUGHT OVER ANOTHER.

William James

2

MINDSET

Mindset is key to understanding why you take on more than is sustainable. In the moment, how you view a situation can affect your feelings and push you closer towards burning out.

By tuning in to your mindset, you can then choose to act in a way that will be more sustainable for your productivity, wellbeing, and mental health.

MINDSET 101: THE BASICS

1 Mindset is key in burnout. The way you think influences how you feel. In turn, it affects your motivation to act. It can push you to do too much, or lead you to avoid things altogether.

2 Mindset includes unhelpful thinking styles, interpretations, expectations, justifications, and attitudes.

3 How you think is affected by emotion and cognitive biases. These shape what you pay attention to, how you interpret a situation, and what you remember.

4 Mindset can be robust, even if it is unhelpful. Over years (or decades) of practice, it's likely you have become an expert in the way that you think – to the point where these thoughts now seem automatic.

5 When shifting your mindset, start with your expectations and beliefs about yourself, others, and the world. These core beliefs shape how you process the information you encounter each and every day.

6 Shifting your mindset also requires you to cushion the impact of mood and cognitive biases. This may require you to focus on the reality of the situation rather than on your interpretation shaped by biases.

7 Unhelpful thinking styles may feel particularly challenging to shift as they are hard to detect. Learn to spot the signs that they are taking over your thoughts and feelings.

8 Shift unhelpful automatic thoughts by learning how to flip your mind's script. Alternatively, adopt a mindfulness approach and accept but not react to these thoughts.

9 Shifting your mindset may seem challenging as you are overriding years of practice in thinking in certain ways. Persistence is the key to change.

UNHELPFUL THINKING STYLES IN BURNOUT

Unhelpful patterns of thinking can lead you down the path of burnout as they bias how you interpret situations and cause you to act in ways that add stress to your life. Which unhelpful thinking styles do you fall prey to?

CATASTROPHISING

Catastrophising about the worst case scenario creates a sense of urgency, and can increase worry and distress. This can result in unhelpful behaviours that lead to burnout.

"I'll lose my job if I don't deliver on this presentation, and my career will be over. I really need to pull an all-nighter to work harder on this."

SHOULDS + MUSTS

Setting inflexible standards can be a recipe for burnout as there's little wiggle room when things don't go according to plan.

"I must prove I'm capable by taking on everything that comes my way."

MIND READING + PREDICTIVE THINKING

Making assumptions about what someone thinks, or about what will happen, without knowing the facts, can lead you down a negative path.

"She thinks I'm incompetent - I can just tell by the way she looked at me. I must work extra hard to prove myself to her."

PERSONALISATION

Here you accept a disproportionate amount of responsibility for outcomes.

"It's all my fault that our team didn't win the project. Even though the competitor's pitch was out of left field, I should've been able to anticipate it."

ALL-OR-NOTHING THINKING

Thinking in rigid absolutes can cause you to unravel if you miss out by a narrow margin.

"I missed out on getting a High Distinction. I must now work twice as hard so that I don't fail again next time."

LABELLING

Taking an action and turning it into a personal failing can contribute to burning out.

"If I'm not constantly busy and being productive then I'm lazy."

NEGATIVE FILTER

Tuning in to the negatives, whilst filtering out positive feedback, can lead to a world of doom and gloom where you are never enough.

"There's always something I could have done better. When will he be satisfied with my work?"

DISCOUNTING THE POSITIVES

Discounting the positives happens when you explain away any successes. Typically, you assign more weight to negative rather than positive feedback.

"I know they said I did a good job, but they were just trying to spare my feelings."

EMOTIONAL REASONING

Feelings aren't facts, but in the face of strong emotions it's easy to believe there's truth behind the way that you feel.

"I know I've prepared for this exam but I don't feel ready. I must've missed something. I'll have to keep studying until it feels right."

UNHELPFUL THINKING STYLES

Halt **mind reading** or **predictive thinking** by seeing it as just *one* possible explanation. It's a guess, not a fact.

"Maybe she isn't thinking that I'm not up to scratch. Maybe she is thinking about something else altogether. She has been distracted of late."

Move away from **all-or-nothing** and instead see progress as incremental. It may also help to acknowledge those successes you have achieved.

"I really wanted a High Distinction, but even though I didn't quite get there doesn't mean I've failed. My mark is still good."

Shift **emotional reasoning** by focusing on facts. Just because something feels a certain way does not make it true. Reflect on times when you've had a hunch that did not come true.

"This happens for every exam that I sit - I get really anxious and am convinced that I'll fail, but I've never actually failed. Realistically, feeling anxious doesn't necessarily mean I will fail. Staying up all night to cram more in at this point won't help."

Stop **catastrophising** by gaining perspective. Step back and look at ALL of the events that need to happen in order for the worst case scenario to occur - what is the realistic probability of all of these events actually occurring? Even if the worst case scenario occurred, would you be able to cope?

"Even if this presentation doesn't go as planned it doesn't mean my career is over. I may not like the outcome, but it's unlikely I'll be fired and my career ruined. My work is otherwise very good."

SHIFTING UNHELPFUL THINKING STYLES

It's helpful to reflect on how unhelpful thinking styles influence your negative thoughts and push you towards burnout. Here are some ways in which to shift the unhelpful thinking patterns that get you unstuck.

Shift **labelling** by focusing on the specific behaviour or event, rather than seeing outcomes as a permanent personality flaw.

"I fell behind on *this* project, but it doesn't mean I'm incompetent. I've delivered many other projects on time and received positive feedback for them."

Loosen the hold of your **shoulds and musts** by counting the costs of your standards. Instead, treat them as preferences, rather than absolutes.

"I'd like to show them I'm capable, but taking on *everything* just isn't realistic nor is it sustainable. It's better to focus on a few things and do them well, rather than burn out trying to do everything perfectly."

Counter **personalisation** by looking at other factors that contribute to the outcome, or reflect on whether you are taking on too much responsibility.

"I would've liked for us to be successful this time around but this was a team effort and we all - not just me - contributed to it."

Balance a **negative filter** by focusing on one positive for every negative that you can think of.

"Yes, he mentioned improvements to make, but those were on selective parts of my project so the rest was likely okay."

Stop **discounting the positives** by anchoring it to objective feedback. You can also step outside of your own mind and reflect on what feedback you'd give someone who achieved the same goal. We're often too quick to squash our own achievements but wouldn't dream of letting a good friend do the same.

"Yes, he could've just said it to be nice, but I did also receive positive feedback from other people who were present."

Discounting is an unhelpful thinking style that is particularly damaging for burnout because it dismisses accomplishments and leads you to believe that you must keep pushing hard to achieve success.

Burnout arises because discounting breeds a 'never good enough' mentality - you rarely feel like you've succeeded, and the value of your achievements is downplayed as successes that could be achieved by anyone. This pattern of thinking is commonly seen in perfectionism and imposter syndrome, and the consequence is a pattern of constantly working harder and taking on more in order to prove your worth.

If discounting is something that you do, perhaps it's time to re-evaluate how well it is serving your self-esteem, wellbeing, quality of life, and burnout.

HOW DISCOUNTING LEADS TO BURNOUT

Discounting serves to diminish the value of your achievements **when a task feels easy or when you're successful**. Thoughts such as "They set the bar too low" and "Anyone could've done it" devalues objectively significant achievements.

This is commonly seen in imposter syndrome, where you fail to internalise objective achievements. The main question to ask yourself is how is it possible that you have managed to fool everyone and every objective test to miraculously land where you are today?

When a task feels challenging or if a setback is experienced, discounting of your skill and ability can easily set in. The belief that "If a task is hard it means I'm not good enough" fails to take into account the context in which the task was performed.

Is it possible that the task was designed to challenge you and extend your skillset? If you went through life only doing things you already knew, then you would not be learning and growing.

Is it possible that you are also discounting the context surrounding the task? It's easy to overlook constraints that you face, instead believing that outcomes reflect only your abilities and not the circumstances.

Finally, did your own expectations and unrealistic goal-setting lead you to take on more than is realistically achievable, thereby setting you up to fail?

When someone praises you, dismissing their intentions with thoughts such as "They were only being nice" only creates a no-win situation. You either feel bad about no one recognising your worth, or you reject any positive feedback that comes your way.

Do you compare yourself to others and feel bad? Measuring your warts-and-all life against someone's highlights reel can lead to burnout as you:

- Work harder to perform like your colleague who doesn't juggle as many commitments as you do.
- Train for hours after a long day at your desk to keep as fit as your personal trainer friend.
- Party harder so you have an Insta-worthy life like your friends (when, really, you'd rather be at home).

What's the solution? Try the following:

- **Question what you are consuming.** Are you seeing a fleeting, filtered moment in time rather than what happens in real life?
- **Consider context.** What lies behind the highlights reel that you see? Is it possible it's not as easy or effortless as you imagine it to be?
- **Focus on your goals and values.** Avoid falling prey to shiny object syndrome and green-eyed monsters.

SOCIAL COMPARISON

THE GRASS ISN'T GREENER ON THE OTHER SIDE. IT'S GREENER  WHERE YOU WATER IT.

SELF COMPASSION

how showering your mind with kindness helps burnout

What is self-compassion?

Self-compassion is showing yourself the same kindness you would to loved ones in challenging times. It is particularly powerful against the self-criticism that pushes so many towards burnout.

Psychologist Kristin Neff outlines three components of self-compassion:

- **Self-kindness** where you show kindness to yourself when you make a mistake or find things challenging. This involves being kind rather than critical, and acknowledging that you are doing the best that you can.
- **Common humanity** recognises that everyone makes mistakes and that suffering is a universal experience - you are not alone.
- **Mindfulness** of negative thoughts and emotions such that you may feel the effects of setbacks but do not attach your identity to them.

Self-compassion + burnout

Studies show that self-compassion is linked to lower levels of burnout, particularly its emotional exhaustion component. It has also been linked to greater job satisfaction, better quality of life, and improved sleep.

When to use self-compassion

You can use self-compassion at any time, and particularly so when:

- You make a mistake.
- You see flaws in yourself.
- You aren't able to reach the goals that you set for yourself.
- You criticise yourself.
- You face challenging situations or feel overwhelmed.
- You want to deny or invalidate your negative feelings.

Over the page are exercises that you can use in these moments.

When is it helpful for you to show self-compassion?

Self-compassion mindset exercises

- **Practise mindfulness of self-critical thoughts.** Accept the experience of negative thoughts (and feelings) as they are, without fighting them. Approach them with curiosity rather than judgement.
- **Acknowledge you are not alone in your pain and suffering.** Setbacks happen in life, and people make mistakes. You are not alone in your experience - it is human to be imperfect and life is not perfect.
- **Write a self-compassionate letter.** Think of a difficult situation or something you feel inadequate about. Write yourself a letter from the perspective of an imaginary friend who cares for you unconditionally and accepts your strengths and weaknesses. In this friend's voice, from a place of kindness, write this letter supporting you in your experience. What does this friend say to you?
- **Practise loving-kindness meditation** in which you let go of self-judgement and self-criticism, tune in to the universal experience of pain and suffering, and direct kindness towards yourself.

Other ways in which you can show yourself some self-compassion include:
- Self-compassion imagery
- Practising self-care
- Supportive touch
- Self-compassion break

> What self-compassion mindset shifts will you make?

THIS IS WHAT COMPASSION DOES.

IT CHALLENGES OUR ASSUMPTIONS, OUR SENSE OF SELF-LIMITATION, WORTHLESSNESS, OF NOT HAVING A PLACE IN THE WORLD, OUR FEELINGS OF LONELINESS AND ESTRANGEMENT.

Sharon Salzberg

FIXED vs GROWTH MINDSET

Mindset is a powerful thing, especially when it tells you what you can and can't do. Self-limiting mindsets such as a fixed mindset see success and failure as a result of an innate ability - you either have it or you don't. In contrast, a growth mindset views ability as something that can be developed through learning and practice. Those with a growth mindset are less concerned with looking capable than they are about learning.

A growth mindset is linked to higher wellbeing levels and improved performance. It is also a more self-compassionate view of achievement. The differences between fixed and growth mindsets are highlighted on the next page. Which mindset do you identify with?

FIXED MINDSET

What it is
A fixed mindset sees ability as innate and endowed at birth – you either have it or you don't.

In the face of challenges
Challenges are seen as threats and tests of your ability (and worth). If you don't believe you can do something, you might be more inclined to avoid potential failure.

Applying effort
When you have a fixed mindset, the idea of needing to work at something may been seen to reflect failure and incompetence.

Coping with setbacks
Whether it's criticism or obstacles, setbacks are seen as a sign of failure and a reflection that you don't have what it takes to succeed. As a result, you may give up altogether.

Reacting to others' successes
Social comparison can be unhealthy for fixed mindsets as they may feel threatened by the success of others.

GROWTH MINDSET

What it is
A growth mindset sees ability as something that can be developed through learning and practice.

In the face of challenges
Challenges are seen as opportunities to learn and stretch yourself. You don't expect to know the answers because you haven't previously encountered the question.

Applying effort
In a growth mindset effort is expected if you are aiming to achieve something new. It reflects neither incompetence nor failure.

Coping with setbacks
Setbacks are viewed as opportunities to learn and refine knowledge and skill. Because of this mindset, you are more likely to persist with the task at hand.

Reacting to others' successes
The success of others is an opportunity to learn and to be inspired. There is admiration rather than jealousy.

FLIP THE SCRIPT

shift your mindset to reduce your burnout

What's your script?

Given the importance of mindset on feelings and actions, if you are to shift burnout it helps to first understand what your script is. That is, how do all of the elements of mindset - expectations, beliefs, interpretations, thinking styles, and attitudes - manifest around events that push you to do too much? Here are some moments to consider:

Before an event
- What expectations do you have about your ability in this instance (fixed vs. growth)?
- Do you have negative beliefs about the event? What about negative beliefs about the outcome?

During the event
- Do you pay selective attention to information that is congruent with your concerns, and ignore what isn't?
- Do you interpret events in a manner congruent with your beliefs and expectations?

After the event
- Do you accept all types of feedback, or only negative ones that reinforce your beliefs about yourself, the task, or the outcome?
- Does this outcome reinforce your view of yourself, others, and the world, or does it shift your expectations and beliefs?

Ty

Due to wanting to be liked by others and fearing rejection by them, Ty worries about displeasing his friend at dinner. He spends the dinner discussing safe and inoffensive topics, all whilst watching for signs that his friend is not having an enjoyable time. He interprets her frown as disapproval of the dinner. Afterwards, Ty blames himself for not being a good friend - if he was he would be more attuned to her likes and dislikes, and she would have had a nicer time.

How to flip the script

1

Identify your negative script
It's easy to notice when you have a negative script – the first sign is often a negative feeling. When this occurs, reflect on the following:
- What was going through your mind immediately before you felt that way?
- What do those thoughts say about you, others, and the world?
- What impact did those thoughts have on your burnout?

2

Question your script
Rather than assume your negative script is correct, play detective:
- What evidence is there that supports your script? What about evidence that contradicts your script?
- If an objective observer was looking in, what would they see?
- If you were less self-critical, what would your script be?
- Are you ruminating on a situation that has no solution?
- What is the cost of thinking this way?
- What unhelpful thinking styles are biasing your script? (To shift specific thinking styles, refer to the earlier section on this topic.)

3

Rewrite your script
Having questioned your script, rewrite it so that it is more balanced and takes into account the negatives and positives in the scenario. This is not intended to be a glib statement that glosses over your challenges or struggles – if it is to have a real impact on your mood it has to be balanced and believable.

Ty

Ty can question and rewrite his script by recognising that it was his friend who contacted him to catch up. He recalls that she frowned when talking about a frustrating issue at work. His friend also said she had a great time and apologised for talking about work. Altogether, his fear of rejection was unfounded.

Flip your script

Think of a recent situation where you experienced overwhelm or burnout. Following the steps in 'How to flip the script', rewrite your unhelpful self-talk.

Flip the script on imposter syndrome

If you suffer from imposter syndrome here are our tips to help you flip the script. Below are some prompts to help you see yourself in a different light and turn down the volume on the imposter within.

See yourself through another person's eyes.

Sure, you might discount your achievements, but if you could see yourself through someone else's kinder eyes, what would you notice?

Test your thoughts by reining in over-preparation.

The problem with over-preparation is that it becomes the explanation for your achievement (and leads to burnout too!). Is it possible that you might do a good enough job with an appropriate level of effort? Choose one task, spend a reasonable (not excessive) amount of time working on it, and notice the impact it has on burnout in relation to how you feel.

Flip the script on imposter syndrome

Flip your unhelpful script.

Irrespective of which type of imposter syndrome you experience, unhelpful self-talk most certainly maintains feeling like a fraud. Perhaps it's time to shift:

- The 'Perfectionist' with their unrealistic standards would do well to see deviations from unrealistic standards as reflecting the unrealistic expectations themselves, rather than ability.

- The 'Expert' may desire to know everything about a topic, but this isn't sustainable. It may help to underscore the commitment to lifelong learning, which goes hand in hand with feeling less than an expert when encountering a new topic.

- The 'Soloist' may benefit from recognising that most successful individuals have a support team behind them.

- The 'Natural Genius' can help their imposter syndrome by recognising that it's rare to succeed on the first attempt when learning something new. Instead, mastery requires learning and practise.

- The 'Superhero' may wish to do everything exceptionally well, however given the number of commitments they take on is it realistic to expect everything to be completed to the same exacting standards?

All types of imposters would also do well to rein in discounting of positive feedback and minimising their focus on negative feedback. So, what shifts do you need to make?

Flip the script on perfectionism

Perfectionism is something that you may have carried for years, or even decades. Why does perfectionism exist? Largely because it has, in some ways, gotten you where you are today. As such, it can be challenging to flip the script on perfectionism for the following reasons:

- Perfectionism is typically underpinned by a fear of not being good enough or of being incompetent in a domain that is important to you.

- Perfectionism, unrealistic expectations, and unrelenting standards often go hand in hand. When these standards aren't met, failure is internalised (rather than attributed to the unrealistic standards). When these standards are met (often at a great cost to time and/or effort), they are then discounted as being easy to achieve (since you were able to achieve them), and you end up in search of a more worthy (a harder and more unrealistic) goal.

- Unhelpful thinking styles abound in perfectionism. In addition to discounting the positives:
  - Thinking in shoulds and musts underpin the rigid and unrelenting standards seen in perfectionism.
  - An all-or-nothing thinking style means that any deviation, however small, is seen as failure. There may also be a tendency to focus on signs of failure (negative filter).
  - There is often emotional reasoning at play - that is, treating feelings as facts - as you wait for moments when it feels 'just right' or 'good enough' before stopping a task.

- With the negative mindset that places increased pressure to perform, it's not surprising that perfectionism is linked to procrastination. Unfortunately, the problem is only delayed, and may even reinforce unhelpful beliefs around being lazy or unproductive (and reinforcing feelings of inadequacy).

Flip the script on perfectionism

Emily juggles her part time job with a young family and excelled at everything she attempted, relishing a high degree of control over the tasks she undertakes. Now that she has taken on an extra role (parenting), the 'struggle of the juggle' leads her to feel like a failure.

Recently, Emily threw a birthday party for one of her children at a time when she was extremely busy at work. Hours were spent on social media researching how to make the best themed cake and party food, as well as decorations. On the day of the party, Emily felt frazzled as the event flew by in a hazy of busyness, and she felt guilty that she did not get to celebrate the party properly with her children.

1 Identifying Emily's negative script

Emily recognised that because the party didn't feel as relaxed and enjoyable that she felt like a failure. She felt incompetent because the party food, birthday cake, and decorations did not look like they did on social media. She also felt like a bad parent because she did not properly celebrate with her children.

2 Questioning Emily's script

Emily reflected on her experiences of the day, on the experiences of others who have been in her situation, and on her thoughts and thinking styles. She remembered that her friends noted that children's parties tended to be busy and focused on running party games, decorating, cooking, handing out party bags, and feeding everyone at the party.

She also reflected on the social media accounts that she followed, and these accounts happened to be run by party planners, chefs, and pastry chefs.

3 Rewriting Emily's script

After questioning her script, Emily realised that she was benchmarking her efforts against professionals which was unrealistic. She also took on board her friends' feedback that children's parties required a lot of effort and preparation, which would likely lead to feeling frazzled. However, this was not a reflection of failure on her part but instead on the scope of the task.

Flip the script - Will

Will's company is tendering for a project in an area they have limited experience in but wish to expand into. With his Mr Fix-It reputation at work, everyone is looking to him to have the answers. Will thinks:

"This is going to be a complete disaster. They think I know enough to secure this project! And I should given I'm Mr Fix-It. If I don't get this right everyone will know I'm a fraud. I'll be laughed at by everyone and they'll lose respect for me."

"There's no way I will let myself be embarrassed like this. I'll have to pull a few all-nighters in order to prove myself. My reputation depends on it."

Questioning Will's script

All-or-nothing thinking
Labelling
Predictive thinking
Catastrophising
Mind reading
Shoulds and musts

Will has worked in this company for decades, and given that this is a new area for them, he has rarely encountered this topic and hence his knowledge would be limited.

Will reflected and felt that this would be an exciting opportunity to learn new things.

Flip the script

"I know we want to move into this field, but there's a lot of knowledge for us to get our heads around given we haven't done much in this area. It's unrealistic to expect that I'll know this information without doing research, and I know my colleagues are aware of this."

"We can use this as a learning experience and learn together. Even if we don't win this project we'll be better prepared for similar projects in the future."

Flip the script - Heni

Heni is keen to make a good impression. Her manager asks if she would like to be involved in a project, acknowledging that whilst Heni has a lot on her plate work-wise she may still find it interesting. Heni reflects on the request.

"Surely this is a test - my manager thinks I'm incompetent. I must say yes. She expects me to take the project on to prove myself, and I don't want to miss out on a chance like this."

"I must prove myself and show my manager that I can perform in spite of a heavy workload. I have to show her that I'm good enough."

Questioning Heni's script

Predictive thinking
Catastrophising
Mind reading
Shoulds and musts

Heni's manager is already aware of Heni's workload and asked for availability, rather than just assign her the project.

Heni reflected and felt flattered her manager thought she might be able to take on more in spite of an already heavy workload.

Flip the script

"I'd *really* like to work on this project. Yet as much as I want to, I'm already overloaded with other projects. Realistically I don't think they're testing me - if they didn't think my work was decent they wouldn't have given me the projects that they have."

"I can thank my manager for offering the opportunity to me and explain that, as she mentioned, I do have a few projects on at the moment, and to keep me in mind for other upcoming projects. In doing so, I am showing that I can prioritise my workload."

Flip the script - Ali

Ali is an extremely conscientious student and marks are everything to him. He feels extremely anxious as exams are coming up, to the point where he is panicking. This leads him to procrastinate in his studies.

"This is so awful. I'm so anxious about the exams - I'm going to fail, I can just feel it! If I fail it'll be the end of my career before it's even begun! I'll have to repeat this year and others will think poorly of me. I'm such an idiot."

"I'd better stay up all night to study. That way the information will stay in my memory right up until the exam starts. I can't stop studying until I feel certain that I know everything."

Questioning Ali's script

All-or-nothing thinking
Labelling
Predictive thinking
Catastrophising
Mind reading
Emotional reasoning

Ali sees that catastrophising only increases his anxiety and cutting down on sleep will harm his memory and concentration.

He also recognises that whilst he feels anxious this is exactly how he feels prior to every exam (and he has not failed any exams).

Flip the script

"I just need to get 63% to achieve the grade that I want. In reality, it's the same pattern each exam - I get so anxious and panicky and I still pass. So, my anxiety does not predict my test result."

"If I keep catastrophising about this I will lose sleep and won't be fresh for the exam. Catastrophising also means I'll be so overwhelmed that I'll procrastinate anyway."

"I'll work on getting enough sleep, reading my notes one last time, and practise mindfulness to help with my anxiety. Everything else I can't really control and I'll have to roll with it."

Flip your script

Think of a recent challenging situation related to your burnout.

Describe the situation below, and the thoughts you experienced in relation to this situation.

Questioning your script

What unhelpful thinking styles are at work? List these below.

Next, question your script:

Flip the script

Finally, flip your script based on your questioning of your script.

3

ACTIONS

Actions play an important part in the burnout landscape. What you choose to do can either keep you stuck on Planet Burnout, or help you revitalise it. So, which path will you choose?

This section covers those actions that impact on burnout and the steps you can take to better manage it.

LIFESTYLE FACTORS

Burnout is often linked to lifestyle factors such as sleep, diet, exercise, and alcohol. Choices you make in these areas can add more strain to an already stretched system.

This section looks at small steps you can take to address the impact of your lifestyle choices on burnout. We also look at how to slow down when life gets too overwhelming.

MANAGING YOURSELF

How you manage yourself and your routine also affects burnout. There are ways to better manage your time and energy to reduce burnout, and this may include putting systems into place, learning to prioritise your workload, and setting boundaries so you can limit your workload to protect your wellbeing.

LIFESTYLE +BURNOUT

When it comes to burnout, an all-too-familiar pattern is one where you face significant time pressure and workload, and the way you catch up on this is to work longer hours. This can leave you physically and psychologically drained.

Too often the solution is to scrimp on sleep, exercise, nutrition, and self-care - these are seen to take time away from your To Do list. Unfortunately, by neglecting these, you end up exacerbating the burnout problem. This section outlines practical lifestyle steps you can take to recover from burnout.

WE NEED TO DO A
BETTER JOB

OF PUTTING OURSELVES
HIGHER

ON OUR OWN
'TO DO' LIST

Michelle Obama

You ride the high of caffeine, in addition to cortisol + adrenaline from the challenges of the day.

Mornings can feel like a struggle after a poor night of sleep, leading you to reach for caffeine to kick start your day.

YOUR DAILY

Are you stuck on a rollercoaster of highs and lows when it comes to energy levels? Sluggish starts in the mornings are masked by a jolt of caffeine until adrenaline and cortisol take over as the day progresses. Then, when your energy levels dip, to

The rest of the day brings more challenges and, with that, stress.

Feeling tired but wired, you reach for something to dull your mind; often alcohol or mind-numbing activities.

Your energy dips, and to get through the remainder of the day you reach for sugar and caffeine.

ROLLERCOASTER

get through the rest of the day you reach again for caffeine or sugar to pick you up. By the evening you may find it hard to wind down and turn to mind-numbing activities or alcohol. You may even stay up late (yes, bedtime procrastination is a thing!), thereby making the next day feel even more of a struggle.

WHY SLEEP MATTERS

sleep + emotions

Sleep affects your ability to regulate emotions, and sleep deprivation has been linked to increased irritability, anxiety, and depression. Indeed, sleep has been found to contribute to the emotional exhaustion component of burnout.

sleep + health

Adequate sleep supports optimal health, which in turn supports your performance.

When you sleep your body repairs itself so that it is ready to face another day.

sleep + performance

Ever scrimped on sleep in order to get on top of your workload? Unfortunately, this has the undesirable effect of harming your performance.

A lack of sleep can affect situational awareness, concentration, judgement, and reaction time. Indeed, sleep deprivation has been implicated in accidents on the road and in rail.

Creativity and problem-solving also take a back seat when you're tired as it becomes easier to revert to old ways of thinking and doing.

Feeling tired and irritable can also lead you to react and communicate in unhelpful ways, so if your role involves interacting with others, consider what impact a lack of sleep is having.

factors affecting sleep

By understanding some basics about sleep you can take steps to get a better night of sleep. Here we focus on three factors you can influence to get a better night of sleep.

sleepiness, caffeine + naps

Adenosine is a neurotransmitter that affects sleep. When you are awake, adenosine builds up to a point where you feel sleepy. Adenosine levels are reduced when you sleep.

Naps in the late afternoon or evening affect sleepiness at bedtime as there is an insufficient build up of adenosine. Caffeine also interferes with the effects of adenosine and thus sleepiness.

sleep stages + alcohol

There are five sleep stages - four non-REM stages, followed by REM sleep. Deep sleep (stages 3 and 4) is when the body repairs itself, and when memory is consolidated. REM sleep is linked to problem-solving.

These stages last around 90-120 minutes, meaning you experience around four or five cycles each night.

Alcohol may send you off to sleep sooner, but it interferes with deep sleep and REM sleep, leaving you feeling unrefreshed.

The body has an internal clock that is sensitive to levels of light shining on the retina.

At dusk, lower levels of light leads to the release of melatonin, which promotes sleepiness.

Artificial light (from globes and devices) suppresses melatonin production, and disrupts your sleep-wake cycle.

light + your circadian rhythm

SLEEP ESSENTIALS

A GOOD NIGHT'S SLEEP
starts in the morning

morning
- Have a consistent wake time (yes, even on weekends!).
- Seek out light to help regulate your circadian rhythm.
- Exercise. It helps you to relax and promotes sleep at night.
- If you consume caffeine, try to have it earlier in the day.

afternoon + early evening
- Do some light exercise.
- Do your 'brain dump' for the day; set up your To Do list for tomorrow.
- Limit naps late in the day as they may interfere with sleepiness at night.
- Eat a light meal to aid digestion.
- Limit alcohol consumption.
- Limit use of stimulants such as nicotine and caffeine.

time to wind down
- Limit blue light/devices that interfere with sleepiness.
- Shift to non-electronic activities such as reading a book or tidying up.
- Set up routine for the next day - meal prep, gather equipment.
- Limit your intake of fluids.
- Have a warm shower.
- Write in your journal or gratitude diary.
- Wind down with relaxation, meditation, or mindfulness.
- Limit intensive exercise so you aren't overly stimulated.

bedtime
- Ensure your room is sufficiently warm, dark, and quiet.
- Move your clock out of sight if clock-watching is an issue for you.
- Place devices out of sight and out of reach.
- Shift unhelpful self-talk that places pressure on falling asleep.
- Practise meditation and mindfulness to extend a relaxed feeling.

WHAT IS BEDTIME PROCRASTINATION?

Ever have that feeling where you're tired as anything but still stay awake in spite of knowing the negative effects it'll have on you the next day? You're not alone. Bedtime procrastination is a thing. Read on to find out more.

THE TALES YOU TELL YOUR SLEEPY SELF

Justifications, bargaining, and seemingly irrelevant decisions – do any of the following sound familiar when it comes to why you procrastinate on your bedtime?

"I'm on a roll! I can't stop now!"

"This is the only time I get to myself, and I deserve to enjoy it!"

"I do my best work at night!"

"I'll watch just the start of this. I can always switch it off and go to bed whenever I want."

WHAT'S THE COST?

It's helpful to count the cost of bedtime procrastination. How well do you function and feel the next day?

BEDTIME PROCRASTINATION

EXERCISE

The benefits of exercise when it comes to stress has been well-documented, with studies showing exercise to improve mood, boost wellbeing, as well as enhance the ability to cope with stress.

Exercise has also been linked to lower occupational stress, a better quality of life, as well as a decreased incidence of burnout.

In spite of this, exercise is often one of the first things to fall by the wayside when people start to feel stressed.

If this is you, increase exercise in small amounts. Something is better than nothing, so try:

- Walking during your lunch break (even if it is around the block).
- Moving more. Park your car further away, take the stairs rather than the lift, or alight at an earlier bus stop.
- Having a walking meeting.

Committing to even just 30 minutes a day of exercise is a step in the right direction.

How does diet impact on burnout? Burnout is often experienced by those with high workloads and an intense pace of work, so consider how you will fuel your energy levels. Riding the sugar and caffeine roller coaster may provide a temporary solution, but it will wear you down in the longer term.

Whilst it is one thing to know that a healthy diet helps, it's another entirely to stick to one. When you are time-poor and regularly feel exhausted, convenience often determines your food choices, so try the following tips:

- Choose healthier options on the menu if you are having takeaway.
- Opt for foods that require less preparation. Bananas and apples, or buying fruit salad, are easier to grab options and therefore remove an obstacle to a healthier diet.
- Select snacks that sustain your energy levels throughout the day so you aren't on the caffeine and sugar roller coaster.

DIET

ALCOHOL

Taking the edge off a long day with alcohol may seem like a good idea (wine o'clock anyone?), but is it making the next day even harder for you?

Find alcohol-free ways to wind down (try a hobby or meditation), count your drinks, or consider low-alcohol options.

Consider swapping catch ups with friends for an occasional alcohol-free one.

ILLICIT USE OF DRUGS

Along with alcohol, the illicit use of drugs (including the misuse of prescription drugs) is an unhelpful way of coping with burnout that does not address its underlying causes.

LIFESTYLE VICES

SEDENTARY LIFESTYLE

An inactive lifestyle - where you spend hours sitting whilst working or studying, and engaging in sedentary leisure activities (such as gaming, watching tv) - is linked to burnout.

Find ways to get moving, be standing rather than sitting, taking the stairs rather than the lift, and choosing leisure activities that get you moving.

NICOTINE

Whilst smokers may light up when they feel stressed and overwhelmed, nicotine actually adds to the stress on the body.

SLOW DOWN

what you can gain by going slow

what's the hurry?

What is the point of rushing?
Of squeezing everything into your day?
Of feeling drained and exhausted.
Of feeling unfulfilled.

Where are you going?
Will it be enough when you get there?

Slow down.
Slow down for your health.
Slow down for your wellbeing.
Slow down just because.

Be mindful.
Be present.
Enjoy moments.

1 Slow down your breathing rate and start to feel calmer. Take three deep breaths, and exhale slowly.

2 Unplug and free yourself from being a slave to your devices.

10 ways to

3 Get out in nature and soak in your surroundings. Tune in to the sights, sounds, and smells of your environment.

4 Say no to the one extra thing you planned on squeezing into your day. Use this time instead to take things at a slower pace. Relax, connect, or just do nothing.

5 Take time to connect with loved ones. Really connect. Set aside distractions and listen.

6 Slow down and watch the world pass by.

7 Savour moments. Whether it's your lunch, or time with your child, maximise your pleasure from each moment.

8 Meditate. It compels you to slow right down. Whether it's mindfulness meditation, loving kindness meditation, or progressive relaxation, these can all help you to take things at a slower pace. Use an app to help.

slow down

9 Do one thing at a time. Multi-tasking isn't making you more effective, just more frazzled.

10 Journal about your day. Pause and reflect on things you're grateful for.

MINDFULNESS + BURNOUT

Mindfulness is about being in the present moment, tuning in to your surroundings and all senses, focusing on the here and now. It's about paying attention to your experiences without judgement.

It's particularly helpful for minds that fixate on the problems of the future or the failures of the past – these are often problems that are beyond your control. Mindfulness can help you to untangle from these concerns.

Benefits of mindfulness

01 Decreased stress + burnout

02 Increased focus + attention

03 Reduced anxiety + depression

04 Improved physical health

05 Improved quality of life

> FEELINGS
> COME AND GO
> LIKE CLOUDS
> IN A WINDY SKY.
> CONSCIOUS BREATHING
> IS MY ANCHOR.
>
> *Thich Nhat Hanh*

Ways to get mindful

Mindfulness meditation apps like Headspace and Smiling Mind are what most think of when it comes to mindfulness. Here are some other ways to be mindful:

01 Mindful eating

02 Mindful breathing

03 Mindful hobbies

04 Present-moment awareness

05 Mindfulness-based stress reduction

IN THE MOMENT

ON BEING
MINDFUL

Being mindful might sound simple - be in the present moment, tune in to your surroundings, focus on the here and now, and don't judge your experience.

In reality it can be far more challenging - your mind wanders and gets distracted by worries about the future, about the past, and bright shiny things. Strong emotions can also take you off-track. This is common and part of practising mindfulness. When this occurs, try the following:

1. Notice when your mind has wandered
2. Accept the thought without judgement
3. Dismiss the thought
4. Return your attention to your target

YOU CAN'T STOP THE WAVES BUT YOU CAN LEARN TO SURF.

Jon Kabat-Zinn

MANAGING

How you manage yourself can make a big difference to your burnout. When you set yourself an unrealistic To Do list and fail to manage your time and energy appropriately you end up feeling overwhelmed by it all.

YOURSELF

By developing systems that work for you, setting boundaries with others and yourself, and setting realistic goals that you can achieve, you set yourself up for success without the distress.

SELF-SABOTAGING BEHAVIOURS

ARE YOU GUILTY?

Self-sabotaging behaviours are those actions that interfere with you attaining your goals and cause you difficulties in life.

Self-sabotaging behaviours usually either seek to annihilate the problem altogether (being 'extra'), or seek to avoid the negative emotions linked to the issue.

Read on to learn more about self-sabotaging behaviours and how to help.

NOT ASKING FOR HELP

Perfectionists and those with imposter syndrome (particularly 'Soloists'), heed this warning – by avoiding asking for help you are effectively increasing your workload and heading further down the path to burnout.

Asking for help isn't a sign of failure. Particularly when undertaking a new task, you really don't know what you don't know, and asking someone who does could save you hours of angst.

OVERCOMMITTING

Saying yes to something new when you're already stretched to the limit is a recipe for burnout.

Before you next commit, work out what else is on your plate.

BEING OVERLY EXTRA

Being overly extra leads to burnout as you spend unnecessary time on a task when it could be spent on something else on your To Do list.

This could look like spending time making your notes look perfect, or checking the final copy of your assignment eight times.

WAITING FOR THE 'JUST RIGHT' MOMENT

Waiting until something 'feels' right – to start a task or to finish a task, is a hallmark of perfectionism. This can lead to spending too much time on a task, or excessively checking your work.

If you rely on feelings to guide your actions, shift to using objective criteria to know when to stop, for example only checking the final draft twice (rather than ten times).

ANALYSIS PARALYSIS

Overanalysing or overthinking can lead to burnout because you delay taking action to avoid making an incorrect decision.

Shift analysis paralysis firstly by making a mindset shift (there are pros and cons to every choice), knowing that you are able to make the most out of what you are given. Then, act on ONE viable option – not delaying to choose THE most viable option.

PROCRASTINATION

Whether you procrastinate due to feeling overwhelmed, delay as you wait to be in the right mood or frame of mind, or delay starting a task because the deadline isn't looming, procrastination can add to overwhelm and burnout by creating pressure and stress at a later date.

To curb procrastination, break a larger, more overwhelming task, into smaller chunks that are less overwhelming and therefore easier to make a start on. Schedule these bite-sized chunks for when you are most alert (and less likely to procrastinate).

THE IMPACT OF PERFECTIONISM

By now you've probably worked out that perfectionism is linked to a wide range of self-sabotaging behaviours.

Wanting to be seen to be capable and perfect may mean that you overcommit and take on more than you can reasonably complete, yet still try to be overly extra to demonstrate that you churn out work that is flawless. Wanting to prove yourself may also stop you from asking for help or delegating, which increases your workload.

Feeling overwhelmed by the pressure of your workload and needing to perform well can also lead to analysis paralysis wherein you delay making a choice because you want to make the most suitable one possible. Unfortunately, by procrastinating, you are then increasing time pressure which can lead to burnout. To help, perfectionists can try the following:

- Start with a realistic overview of your existing commitments (use a planner!) and how much time and energy they will consume.

- Be realistic in your time estimation. If you find yourself thinking "I *should* be able to fit it in" then you're probably being optimistic rather than realistic. Say no to yourself.

- Focus on objective time limits rather than waiting for the subjective feeling of 'just right' and stick to these limits.

What self-sabotaging behaviours contribute to, and reinforce, your burnout? What specific steps will you take to shift them?

SHIFTING YOUR SELF-SABOTAGING BEHAVIOURS

JUST SAY NO

when problems setting boundaries leads to burnout

Feeling overwhelmed quickly leads us down the path of burnout.

But why do we feel overwhelmed?

Could it be that problems saying no and setting boundaries causes your overwhelm?

How many of the following sound familiar?

- They way that they ask me makes it so hard to say no!
- They'll think I'm selfish.
- They'll get angry if I don't do it.
- They expect me to do it.
- It's hard to say no to them; they don't listen!
- It's not too inconvenient for me to help them out.
- I can't turn down those puppy-dog eyes.

- This is a great opportunity, I really should take it.
- If I want the job done properly I may as well do it myself.
- No one else put their hand up so I guess it's up to me!
- It'll take even longer to explain how to do it! I may as well just do it myself.
- I have to prove myself.
- I'd feel guilty saying no.
- The others are too busy, so I may as well do it.
- I'm sure I can squeeze it in if I juggle a few things around.

Think about setting boundaries with others.

Think about setting boundaries with yourself!

setting boundaries with others

Setting boundaries will feel uncomfortable at first. Start with smaller boundaries before moving on to larger ones.

Think about what you'll say when setting boundaries. The goal is to stand your ground, not to convince the other person to agree with your point of view.

Pushback may happen and that is okay. You are changing a dynamic and that may ruffle feathers.

Practise, practise, practise. This is a new skill and one that you've likely been avoiding for some time. Practise in front of a mirror, practise in front of a good friend, and record it to see how you come across.

setting boundaries with others

Finding it hard to say NO to others can quickly lead to burnout. On top of your own obligations, you now find yourself taking on extra tasks that you probably don't have time for. So why do you find it difficult to set boundaries with others?

it speaks to your identity

Go back to your identity. Are you someone who likes to be liked? Someone who does not like to 'rock the boat'? Someone who wants to ease others' burdens by helping them out? Someone who sees disagreement as conflict? Taking on too much can often stem from a desire to keep the peace and be liked by others.

you're worried about what others think

Is it realistic that every single person that you meet will have a favourable impression of you? What will you do if someone doesn't show that they approve of you? Is your plan to shift and shape your personality and actions to please the other person? How would that align with your values and what you want from life?

you don't have the skills...yet!

It's easy to think that there's an art to setting boundaries. Many fall into the trap of thinking that they have to convince the other person to see their point of view. The reality is that you just have to get more comfortable with enforcing your boundaries.

you need to ease into facing your fear

Sure you may know *how* to set boundaries, but how do you *feel* about facing your fear? Fear can put people off setting boundaries. The best way to ease into facing your fear is by starting out with 'low stakes' boundary-setting. This could be as simple as saying "no" when a waitperson asks if you wish to upsize your menu order.

setting boundaries with yourself

Setting boundaries with yourself may be even harder than setting boundaries with others. So why is it so tricky to say no to yourself?

you think you're kind of special
Whether you believe you're the only one who knows how to do a task, or that only you can do the job properly, hoarding tasks places you on the path to burnout. Is it time to give others an opportunity to learn so you can reduce your workload in the longer-term?

you can't bring yourself to do less than you think you're capable of
When you see how much is on your To Do list, a reality slap may be in order. Being overly extra, or completing each task until it is perfect, will wear you down. Something has to give. Will it be your unrealistic expectations, or will it be your wellbeing? Saying no doesn't mean you're not capable. Saying no means you're saying yes to a more sustainable life.

you can't let go
Just one more revision, just another bit more to research, or just until it's finally good enough. When you can't set the boundary to let go, you end up inflating your workload and stress. If this is the case, rely on external deadlines (for example, only revising a certain number of times) rather than feelings (such as until it feels 'just right').

setting boundaries with yourself

Just because you can doesn't mean you should.

Think carefully about whether you can give a task the attention it needs *in a sustainable manner* before you commit to it.

Do you value the importance of self-care in ensuring you can work sustainably and not burn out?

what boundaries should you set with yourself?

How much work do you *actually* need to put into a task? Are you spending an excessive amount of time on a task when that time could be better spent elsewhere?

STREAMLINE
building systems + processes to reduce your burnout

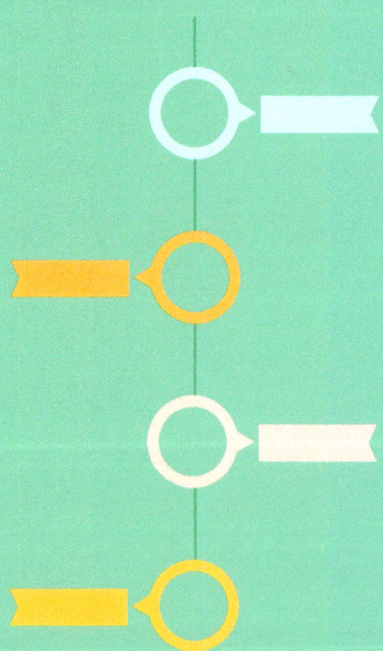

the strain of daily hassles

When it comes stress and burnout, it's easy to overlook the small daily hassles that build up and impact on our quality of life. Do any of the following sound familiar?

- Mornings are a rush to get ready and out the door on time. Challenges may include not having packed your lunch for the day, getting ready when you can't find a matching outfit that is clean, and organising your belongings for the day when you can't find things you've misplaced.

- Navigating your workload for the day. This could mean not prioritising things for completion for the day, forgetting how to complete a task because you do it infrequently, or dealing with the multiple emails and messages that you receive.

- The evening run, including deciding on what to make for dinner, finding time to exercise, doing housework, ensuring that you and those you look after are organised for the next day, completing life admin, socialising... the list goes on.

These seemingly minor daily hassles all add up, affect your quality of life, and contribute to burnout. So how can you better manage them and make your day run smoother?

Enter systems and processes. They may not sound glamourous, but by spending time now to set them up makes your life easier in the longer term. Let's take a closer look at what can be done to ease burnout.

what systems + processes should you set up?

When setting up systems and processes consider those pain points that you experience regularly.

For some it may be the morning rush. For others, it may be a busy work day where juggling multiple demands is the norm. It may also be that life admin takes a toll.

These next sections step through some systems and processes you may wish to consider implementing in your life. The possibilities are endless - use these as a starting point.

*List your **main pain points***

personal systems + processes

Set up systems for the different areas of your personal life to make your days run smoother. Some examples are:

- Cleaning can be a drain and a real hassle. In addition to the necessary daily cleaning, set up a routine where you rotate through other chores in a systematic fashion. This might look like doing laundry on set days, meal prep on another, and vacuuming on a different day.

- Reduce the mental load of meal prep. Set aside time on weekends to plan, shop, and prep for the week ahead. As an added bonus it can also lead to less food wastage and a healthier lifestyle.

- Reduce the 'I have nothing to wear' stress. Ensure outfits are cleaned and ready to wear for the coming week. If coordinating your outfit each morning is a daily hassle, consider building a capsule wardrobe where all items match, or develop your own informal uniform to make mornings easier. Every few months, set aside time to rotate seasonal clothes.

- Set up a system that will help your mornings run smoother. Every night, gather up what you will need for the next day. Pack your bags for work, school, or the gym. Check that any forms or administration due that day have been completed.

work it!

Whatever the nature of your work, there are systems and processes that you could set up to make the day easier.

- Have a system to organise your work flow and workload. Whether this is a timetable, or a To Do list, find a way to gain an overview of your tasks. Map out due dates (and minor due dates) for the weeks ahead.

- Block out times for tasks and limit distractions. Each time you shift attention away from a task it comes at a cognitive cost and reduces your efficiency. Commit to switching off email and other alerts whilst working and instead block out dedicated time to attend to these alerts.

- Document your work processes, in particular for tasks that you perform less frequently. This way, you don't waste time recalling how to perform the task when you encounter it.

- Upskill in those areas that help you implement systems and processes at work with ease. This may include time management skills, communicating assertively, and setting boundaries.

- Develop a system for optimising your performance. This may include having a proper night of rest, setting work priorities each morning, setting limits on work hours, and ensuring self-care is undertaken regularly.

Heni

Heni is a go-getter who spends long hours at work, takes every opportunity that comes her way, and is focused on productivity. Each day is long and feels overwhelming, and alcohol and late nights are constant companions.

- She can start by mapping out all her commitments to gain an overview of her workload.

- Given Heni stays up late and uses alcohol to unwind, she tends to scrimp on sleep and mornings are a struggle. She can make mornings easier by organising herself the night before (set out her clothes, prepare snacks and lunch).

- At work, to maintain focus she could prioritise her tasks each day, and reduce distractions such as email alerts. She can also develop a workflow and set up processes and templates that help her become more efficient.

- After work, and on weekends, focusing on setting herself up for the week can help reduce pressure during workdays. This includes setting aside time to go through processes she has set up for life admin and household chores.

life admin

Life admin - it's the unpaid job you do in addition to your regular role of work, study, or caregiving. Tending to life admin tasks can be tiring as there are multiple tasks in various areas of your life that are never-ending. Below are some examples of life admin tasks, and it is by no means an exhaustive list. If you happen to be responsible for others' life admin (particularly caregivers) then your workload increases.

- **Financial** - Paying bills and fines, managing the household budget, filing taxes, reviewing superannuation, reviewing bank accounts and loans.
- **Social and leisure** - Planning or responding to social events, planning vacations, purchasing gifts, filling in forms for leisure activities (social sports, hobbies, events), responding to messages with friends and family.
- **Health** - Scheduling health appointments, signing up for classes or health-related activities, reviewing health and life insurances.
- **Household** - Attending to mail, managing household supplies, planning meals, organising seasonal maintenance of your property, coordinating IT maintenance, coordinating home improvements, organising maintenance of vehicles.
- **Career** - Completing professional development requirements, updating your resume, maintaining memberships of relevant professional bodies.
- **Personal** - Arranging self-care and personal grooming appointments, sending and replying to personal emails, updating your will.

All of these tasks (and more!) have to be taken care of as ignoring them leads to future stress. Given that these are necessary tasks, adopt an approach to simplify and streamline these as best as possible.

Lay it all out
Write a list of all your life admin tasks, grouping them so you know what needs to be done each day, week, fortnight, month, and year.

Prioritise + declutter
Be discerning with what you spend your time on, and declutter what is not necessary. Set priorities for each day so you don't feel overwhelmed by a long To Do list.

Make room for admin
Diarise time each week for life admin tasks. At certain times of the year consider setting aside extra time for additional tasks such as filing taxes or spring cleaning.

Aim for autopilot
Automating tasks can save you previous time paying bills, sorting emails, and shopping for groceries.

Batch what you can
Grouping tasks that are similar can help you focus better. Paying bills, completing forms, and answering emails are all tasks that can be batched.

Keep a running list
There are always things to buy and do, so keep a running list and add to it as things arise. This helps lighten your mental load.

Find a home
Find a place to house everything. Emails, tools, electronic files, bills, and paperwork - you'll save time each day just by knowing instantly where things are kept.

Upskill to destress
If you procrastinate on life admin because you lack knowledge, spend time learning how to do it so it gets easier over time.

Set reminders
If you regularly hit the snooze button on life admin tasks, try setting reminders as a back up. This way you're doubly sure you stay on track.

WHEN YOU
SOLVE PROBLEMS
AT THE RESULTS LEVEL,
YOU ONLY SOLVE THEM
TEMPORARILY.

IN ORDER TO
IMPROVE FOR GOOD,
YOU NEED TO
SOLVE PROBLEMS
AT THE SYSTEMS LEVEL.

James Clear

your systems and processes

List some systems and processes to develop that will make a difference to your days.

MANAGING TIME + ENERGY

It seems like there are never enough hours in the day to get through your To Do list. Yet pushing through without regard for what you can reasonably sustain for a workload is a recipe for burnout.

So how can you do more when there are only so many hours in a day? As has already been mentioned, scrimping on sleep and self-care only adds to the problem of burnout.

One solution is to work out how to manage your time so that you can maximise what you achieve in a day.

However, managing time goes hand in hand with managing energy. There's a difference between the two - time is finite, but energy ebbs and flows. Need convincing? Consider:

- A difficult phone call may take the same amount of time as messaging a close friend, however one is more emotionally draining than the other.
- Spending half an hour writing your thesis is different from spending half an hour doing housework.

Thus, if you're to recover from burnout and build up your resilience, it's helpful to consider how to better manage your time and energy.

rhythms

When considering managing energy, it's helpful to understand the body's natural rhythms. Two rhythms of significance for managing burnout are circadian rhythm and ultradian rhythm.

Your circadian rhythm is your body's 24-hour internal clock, controlling the sleep-wake cycle. As part of this, there are two peaks of energy and heightened alertness (one occurring a few hours after waking up, and one in the late afternoon) with a dip in energy around 3pm. Certainly, there are individual differences in circadian rhythms that may influence when you are most alert. For example, night owls generally feel most alert much later in the day.

Your ultradian rhythm has a shorter period, lasting about 90-120 minutes, with a peak in energy occurring around 90 minutes, followed by a dip in energy.

Working with, rather than against, these biological rhythms is key to reducing burnout and feeling more energised. Try to align tasks requiring alertness to your peak energy times. For instance, schedule tasks that require focus and concentration for when you're most alert, and save your low energy moments to exercise or practise self-care.

UNDERSTANDING YOUR ENERGY PATTERNS

In addition to aligning tasks on your To Do list with your body's biological rhythms, it's helpful to learn how some activities drain your energy whilst others build it up.

DRAIN

What activities drag down your energy levels?

REGAIN

What activities build up your energy levels?

 Ali

Ali, the student, spends most of his time studying, engages in little self-care and feels disconnected from his friends. Ali spends almost every waking moment focusing on his studies, and is frustrated when he finds it hard to grasp what he is learning. After reflecting on the peaks and troughs of his energy he decides to shuffle his study tasks around so that assignment writing is shifted to when he is most alert.

Ali also recognises that his low energy periods are ideal for building up his energy reserves, for example exercising or socialising. These leave him feeling energised.

WHERE DOES YOUR TIME GO?

Before you go around making changes to your daily routine, let's take a closer look at how you spend your time. Reflect on your past week to see where you spend most of your time.

URGENT + IMPORTANT TASKS
Spending a lot of time in this quadrant can quickly lead to burnout.

NON-URGENT BUT IMPORTANT TASKS
Here you gain traction on necessary tasks, but avoid the pressure of tight deadlines.

URGENT BUT UNIMPORTANT TASKS
These tasks occupy your time but don't mean much in the end.

NON-URGENT + UNIMPORTANT TASKS
Why are you spending time in this quadrant?

MORE QUICK TIPS
TO HELP MANAGE TIME + ENERGY

1 Track what you spend your time and energy on for one week. This helps you identify where your time goes and how different activities affect your energy levels. You can also identify patterns that lead to burnout and areas for change.

2 Accept your reality. What are you unable to shift in your schedule? Often things such as family commitments, or balancing studying with work, are commitments that are difficult to shift even if they take up a lot of your time and energy. Focus on what is within your control to change.

3 Prioritise what's important in your life, and set your schedule accordingly. It's all too easy to get trapped into focusing on things that seem urgent, and to lose sight of what's important. Go back to what you value. Are your actions moving you closer towards what you want to achieve, or are you getting distracted by bright shiny things? Delegate what you can, and put other less important things on the back burner.

4 Understand what's on your radar by using a planner or calendar. Break down tasks into their smaller components, so you can see your upcoming commitments and allocate time and energy accordingly.

5 Align tasks with fluctuations in your energy levels. Focus on tasks that require a lot of energy when you are most alert, and take care of tasks that require less energy when you feel drained. For example, use high energy periods to write a report or have a challenging conversation with a colleague. Use low energy periods to format your report or speak to a good friend.

6 Energising yourself comes in many different forms, including physical, emotional, mental, and spiritual. Choose tasks that build these different energy reserves.
- Increasing physical energy can be as simple as getting enough sleep, nutrition, and exercise. Fuel your body so it can perform well, and take breaks to recharge.
- Build up your mental energy by reducing distractions (turn off email and phone alerts), and cutting down on multitasking.
- Replenish emotional energy using techniques such as shifting your mindset (cognitive restructuring), practising mindfulness meditation, or practising gratitude.
- Increase spiritual energy by focusing on pursuits that give you meaning and purpose.

7 If you plan on sprinting through life, you need time to rest and recover. Consider using the Pomodoro technique where you work intensively for 25 minutes, followed by a five-minute break. After four sprints, take a longer break (15-30 minutes) to recharge.

Alternatively, embrace your ultradian rhythm and work in 90 minute sprints followed by 30 minutes of recovery. It's important to find a system that works for you and your energy levels.

map things out

When it comes to managing your time and energy it's helpful to take an overview of your commitments and to plan ahead so that you are less likely to burn out.

The different areas of your life will make various demands of your time and energy throughout the year, so consider spreading these commitments out if possible.

For Ali, our student, assignment due dates will predictably take time away from studying for exams, so it may help him to spread his study times across the semester to counter this.

 For Emily, who is juggling a young family and work, she may wish to consider planning around school holidays and critical project deadlines at work.

By understanding pressures on her time and energy across a year, Emily can better recognise when to prioritise one over the other, and when to call in additional support.

Over the next pages are planners to help you obtain an overview of your year, month, week, and day. Use these to help you better manage your time and energy so you can reduce burnout.

this year

Month:

this month

monday	tuesday	wednesday	thursday	friday	saturday	sunday

goals

Week commencing:

this week

| monday | tuesday | wednesday | thursday |

| friday | saturday | sunday |

weekly review

healthy habits

mindset magic

what worked? (do more of) **what didn't work?** (change)

Date: M / Tu / W / Th / F / Sa / Su

today

awake

asleep

today's top 3

healthy habits

mindset magic

The **KEY** is not to prioritise what's on your schedule but to **schedule your priorities**

Steven Covey

TAKING ACTION

We've covered a lot of actions that you can take in revitalising Planet Burnout, but how do you know which will be most suitable for you? First of all, it's important not to try everything - that will likely exacerbate your burnout as you attempt to fit everything in to your already-busy schedule.

Instead, be selective in the actions that you choose to change. It all depends on your own circumstances - as you will see below, different circumstances require different approaches. Try a few on for size to see if they can become a sustainable habit in managing your burnout. Let's see what our Planet Burnout inhabitants might choose to do.

Ali

Ali, our student, spends all of his time studying during semester, and feels lonely and disconnected from friends. Perfectionistic in nature, he finds he procrastinates when overwhelmed.

In addition to Ali making a mindset shift that recognises the importance of self-care for optimal performance in his studies, there are a few actions that he can take to help himself.

Lifestyle changes Ali can make include getting enough sleep so that his brain can consolidate learning. He would also benefit from starting to exercise to help his overwhelm - should he worry about 'wasting time', he can consider listening to a podcast on a study topic at the same time. Finally, self-care in the form of relaxation, mindfulness, or connecting with friends will also help his wellbeing.

Ali can better **manage himself** by aligning study tasks and self-care activities to his energy levels. It may also help to set time limits on studying each day. Breaking larger goals into smaller, less daunting ones, can help with his procrastination.

Heni

Heni spends long hours at work, and uses alcohol to unwind, which in turn reinforces her exhaustion and burnout.

In addition to making mindset shifts to strive for a sustainable balance, she can try a few different actions.

Lifestyle changes Heni can make include limiting alcohol consumption, particularly at night when it may affect her sleep and leave her unrefreshed in the morning. Exercise will also help her to cope with the demands of work.

In terms of better **self-management**, Heni could set limits around work, even signing up for a yoga class in the evening twice a week so that she leaves the office by a certain time.

Ty

Wanting to please people means Ty takes on what others ask to the point of neglecting other responsibilities and burning out in the process.

The main mindset shift for Ty is to accept that it is not possible to please everyone, and attempting to do so leads to burnout.

Lifestyle changes for Ty to make include engaging in regular self-care.

In terms of **self-management**, Ty will benefit from setting boundaries with others (assertive communication) and with self (not taking on too much).

ACTION PLAN

WHAT ARE MY GOALS?

WHAT LIFESTYLE CHANGES WILL I MAKE?

HOW CAN I BETTER SELF-MANAGE?

A GOAL
WITHOUT A PLAN
IS JUST A WISH

Antoine de Saint-Exupery

4
OUTCOMES

By changing your mindset and your actions, you choose a different outcome – one that has you feeling less stressed and more resilient.

By continuing to build on these small changes that you make, you can revitalise your burnout and improve your wellbeing.

 Well done on getting started. Sometimes the first step is the hardest. It's all too easy to procrastinate on the 'right' action to take, or worry that you're not doing things correctly, so it's helpful to remember that done is better than perfect.

Change may cause discomfort. When you've been in your comfort bubble for some time (even if you know it leads to burnout) change can feel confronting.

These types of changes may include doing less, which may strike at the core of a perfectionist's identity. It may involve being assertive which will be counter to a people-pleaser's instinct to automatically say yes to everything. If this sounds familiar, it's helpful to count the costs of staying the same (that is, remaining on Planet Burnout) rather than choosing to change.

 Track and reflect on your successes! Rather than dwelling on how much further there is to go (particularly if you're prone to an all-or-nothing thinking style), it's helpful to reflect periodically on how far you've come in relation to feeling better, thinking differently, or doing things differently.

When you've mastered one change, consider what other changes you'd like to make to further build your resilience and revitalise your burnout.

 Focus on making your changes sustainable in the longer-term. By doing so, you are building resilience and cushioning yourself against further burnout (see Section 5 on how to achieve this).

5

BEHAVIOUR CHANGE

Hopefully this workbook has given you a range of reflections and skills to help you revitalise your burnout.

Taking the first step to change can be exciting and fulfilling, but the magic is in sustaining that in the longer term. This section covers the essentials for making changes stick.

1

The changes you are making is akin to learning a new skill - a new way of thinking and a new way of doing. **Skills become easier with practice, so persist with it.** After all, you don't expect to only train once for a marathon and blitz it.

2

Change is not linear. As with all other skills that you have attempted to learn over your lifetime there will be days when you're winning and days when it's harder to get the skill over the line. **Look to your overall progress** to help you maintain motivation through the 'off' days.

3

Circumstances change, and with it you can expect to pivot. Maybe how you're thinking or what you're doing needs only a small adjustment, or maybe it's a chance to build a new skill. Either way, it's helpful to **think of managing burnout as ever-evolving.**

4

Slip ups and setbacks are part of the change process. It's what you do in response to these that matter - you can either opt out of change altogether or you can use it as a learning experience to understand why it occurred, and take steps to do things differently next time.

the right mindset for change

making changes stick

It's one thing to make a change, it's another to make it stick. So how can you make changes sustainable? In *Atomic Habits*, author James Clear outlines the psychological principles behind turning occasional change into longer lasting habits by shaping your environment to decrease or increase a habit's appeal.

Let's say our go-getter Heni wishes to decrease the amount of alcohol she drinks and increase the amount of exercise that she does. Here are some approaches she could take.

increasing exercise	decreasing alcohol
make it obvious Keep gym gear in the car.	**make it invisible** Remove alcohol from house.
make it attractive Buy new gym gear.	**make it unattractive** Channel memories of struggling at work due to a hangover.
make it easy Sign up at a gym close to work.	**make it difficult** If buying alcohol then skip her local and go somewhere far.
make it satisfying Enjoy feeling good.	**make it unsatisfying** For each drink that Heni has, she will buy three rounds for others.

MOTIVATION IS WHAT GETS YOU STARTED.

HABIT IS WHAT KEEPS YOU GOING.

Jim Rohn

tracking your progress

Tracking your progress can really give a sense of satisfaction and achievement. Use the Habit Tracker on the next page to track your progress across a month.

At the end of it, review your progress and see if there are any adjustments to be made for sustained success.

REFERENCES

A TALE OF TWO PLANETS

Alkema, K., Linton, J.M., Davies, R. (2008). A study of the relationship between self-care, compassion satisfaction, compassion fatigue, and burnout among hospice professionals. *Journal of Social Work in End-of-Life & Palliative Care*, *4*(2), 101-119. https://doi.org/10.1080/15524250802353934.

Bressi, S.K., & Vaden, E.R. (2017). Reconsidering self care. *Clinical Social Work Journal*, *45*(1), 33-38. https://doi.org/10.1007/s10615-016-0575-4

Cecil,J., McHale, C., Hart, J., & Laidlaw, A. (2014). Behaviour and burnout in medical students. *Medical Education Online*, *19*:1, https://doi.org/10.3402/meo.v19.25209

Demerouti, E., Mostert, K., & Bakker, A. B. (2010). Burnout and work engagement: A thorough investigation of the independency of both constructs. *Journal of Occupational Health Psychology*, *15*(3), 209-222. https://doi.org/10.1037/a0019408

Devilly, G.J., Wright, R., & Varker, T. (2009). Vicarious trauma, secondary traumatic stress or simply burnout? Effect of trauma therapy on mental health professionals. *Australian & New Zealand Journal of Psychiatry*, *43*(4), 373-385. https://doi.org/10.1080/00048670902721079

Ernst, J., Jordan, K-D., Weilenmann, S., Sazpinar, O., Gehrke, S., Paolercio, F., Petry, H., Pfaltz, M.C., Mean, M., Aebischer, O., Gachoud, D., Morina, N., von Kanel, R., & Spiller, T.R. (2021). Burnout, depression and anxiety among Swiss medical students – A network analysis. *Journal of Psychiatric Research*, *143*,196-201. https://doi.org/10.1016/j.jpsychires.2021.09.017

Gonzalez-Roma, V., Schaufeli, W.B., Bakker, A.B., & Lloretm S, (2006). Burnout and work engagement: Independent factors or opposite poles? *Journal of Vocational Behavior*, *68*(1), 165-174. https://doi.org/10.1016/j.jvb.2005.01.003

Koutsimani, P., Montgomery, A., & Georganta, K. (2019). The relationship between burnout, depression, and anxiety: A systematic review and meta-analysis. *Frontiers in Psychology*, *10*:284, https://doi.org/10.3389/fpsyg.2019.00284

Leiter, M.P., & Maslach, C. (2017). Burnout and engagement: contributions to a new vision. *Burnout Research*, *5*, 55-57. https://doi.org/10.1037/a001940810.1016/j.burn.2017.04.003

Maslach, C. (2011). Burnout and engagement in the workplace: new perspectives. *The European Health Psychologist*, *13*(3), 44-47.

Maslach, C., Schaufeli, W.B., & Leiter, M.P. (2001). Job burnout. *Annual Review in Psychology*, *52*, 397-422.

Parker, G., Tavella, G., & Eyers, K. (2021). *Burnout: A guide to identifying burnout and pathways to recovery*. Allen & Unwin.

Turnipseed, D. L. (1998). Anxiety and Burnout in the Health Care Work Environment. *Psychological Reports*, *82*(2), 627-642. https://doi.org/10.2466/pr0.1998.82.2.627

World Health Organisation, *'Burn-out an "occupational phenomenon": international classification of diseases*. 28 May 2019. https://www.who.int/news/item/28-05-2019-burn-out-an-occupational-phenomenon-international-classification-of-diseases

UNDERSTANDING PLANET BURNOUT

Alarcon, G., Eschleman, K.J., & Bowling, N.A. (2009). Relationships between personality variables and burnout: A meta-analysis. *Work & Stress, 23*(3), 244-263. https://doi.org/10.1080/02678370903282600

Childs, J.H., and Stoeber, J. (2012). Do you want me to be perfect? Two longitudinal studies on socially prescribed perfectionism, stress and burnout in the workplace. *Work and Stress, 26*(4), 347-364. https://doi.org/10.1080/02678373.2012.737547

D'Souza, F., Egan, S., & Rees, C. (2011). The Relationship Between Perfectionism, Stress and Burnout in Clinical Psychologists. Behaviour Change, 28(1), 17-28. https://doi.org/10.1375/bech.28.1.17

Dudau, D.P. (2014). The relation between perfectionism and imposter phenomenon. *Procedia - Social and Behavioral Sciences, 127*, 129-133. https://doi.org/10.1016/j.sbspro.2014.03.226.

Dweck, C. S. (2017). *Mindset: The new psychology of success.* Robinson.

Rosse, J. G., Boss, R. W., Johnson, A. E., & Crown, D. F. (1991). Conceptualizing the Role of Self-Esteem in the Burnout Process. *Group & Organization Studies, 16*(4), 428-451. https://doi.org/10.1177/105960119101600406

Lasalvia, A., Bonetto, C., Bertani, M., Bissoli, S., Cristofalo, D., Marrella, G., Ceccato, E., Cremonese, C., De Rossi, M., Lazzarotto, L., Marangon, V., Morandin, I., Zuchetto, M., & Tansella, M. (2009). Influence of perceived organisational factors on job burnout: Survey of community mental health staff. British Journal of Psychiatry, 195(6), 537-544. https://doi.org/10.1192/bjp.bp.108.060871

Maslach, C. (2011). Burnout and engagement in the workplace: new perspectives. *The European Health Psychologist, 13*(3), 44-47.

Maslach, C., Schaufeli, W.B., & Leiter, M.P. (2001). Job burnout. *Annual Review in Psychology, 52*, 397-422.

Randall, M., & Scott, W.A. (1988). Burnout, job satisfaction, and job performance. *Australian Psychologist, 23*(3), 335-347.

Parker, G., Tavella, G., & Eyers, K. (2021). *Burnout: A guide to identifying burnout and pathways to recovery.* Allen & Unwin.

Sakulku, J., & Alexander, J. (2011). The imposter phenomenon. International Journal of Behavioral Science, 6, 75-97.

Zopiatis, A., & Constanti, P. (2010). Leadership styles and burnout: is there an association?. *International Journal of Contemporary Hospitality Management, 22*(3), 300-320. https://doi.org/10.1108/09596111011035927

REVITALISING PLANET BURNOUT

1. Identity

Antony, M.M., & Swinson, R.P. (1998). *When perfect isn't good enough: Strategies for coping with perfectionism.* New Harbinger.

Clance, P. R., & Imes, S. A. (1978). The imposter phenomenon in high achieving women: Dynamics and therapeutic intervention. *Psychotherapy: Theory, Research & Practice, 15*(3), 241-247. https://doi.org/10.1037/h0086006

Dudau, D.P. (2014). The relation between perfectionism and imposter phenomenon. *Procedia - Social and Behavioral Sciences, 127,* 129-133. https://doi.org/10.1016/j.sbspro.2014.03.226.

Nepon, T., Flett, G.L, Hewitt, P.L., & Molnar, D.S. (2011). Perfectionism, negative social feedback, and interpersonal rumination in depression and social anxiety. *Canadian Journal of Behavioural Science, 43*(4), 297-308. https://doi.org/10.1037/a0025032

Parker, G., Tavella, G., & Eyers, K. (2021). *Burnout: A guide to identifying burnout and pathways to recovery.* Allen & Unwin.

Sakulku, J., & Alexander, J. (2011). The imposter phenomenon. International Journal of Behavioral Science, 6, 75-97.

Vergauwe, J., Wille, B., Feys, M., De Fruyt, F., & Anseel, F. (2014). Fear of being exposed: The trait-relatedness of the imposter phenomenon and its relevance in the work context. Journal of Business Psychology. https://doi.org/10.1007/s 10869-014-9382-5

VIA Institute on Character. *The VIA Character Strengths Survey.* https://www.viacharacter.org/survey/account/register/

Young, V. (2011). *The secret thoughts of successful women: Why capable people suffer from the impostor syndrome and how to thrive in spite of it.* Crown Publishing Group.

2. Mindset

Dweck, C. S. (2017). *Mindset: The new psychology of success.* Robinson.

Edelman, S. (2003). *Change your thinking.* ABC Books.

Eysenck, M.W., & Keane, M.T. (2015). *Cognitive psychology. A student's handbook. (7th ed.).* Psychology Press.

Egan, S.J., Wade, T.D., Shafran, R., & Antony, M.M. (2014). *Cognitive-behavioral treatment of perfectionism.* Guilford Press.

Greenberger, D., & Padesky, C.A. (1995). *Mind over mood: Change how you feel by changing the way you think.* Guilford Publications.

Neff, K. (2003). Self-compassion: An alternative conceptualisation of a healthy attitude toward oneself. *Self and Identity, 2*(2), 85- 101. https://doi.org/10.1080/15298860309032

Richardson, C.M.E., Trusty, W.T., & George, K.A. (2018). Trainee wellness: Self-critical perfectionism, self-compassion, depression, and burnout among doctoral trainees in psychology. *Counselling Psychology Quarterly, 33*(2), 187-198. https://doi.org/10.1080/09515070.2018.1509839

Wheeler, L., & Miyake, K. (1992). Social comparison in everyday life. *Journal of Personality and Social Psychology, 62,* 760-773. https://doi.org/10.1037/0022-3514.62.5.760

3. Actions

Antony, M.M., & Swinson, R.P. (1998). *When perfect isn't good enough: Strategies for coping with perfectionism.* New Harbinger.

Bressi, S.K., & Vaden, E.R. (2017). Reconsidering self care. *Clinical Social Work Journal, 45*(1), 33-38. https://doi.org/10.1007/s10615-016-0575-4

Burdick, D., (2013). *Mindfulness skills workbook for clinicians and clients.* PESI Publishing & Media.

Covey, S. (2004). *The 7 habits of highly effective people. Pocket Books.*

Davis, D.M., & Hayes, J.A. (2011). What are the benefits of mindfulness? A practice review of psychotherapy-related research. *Psychotherapy, 28,* 198-208. https://doi.org/10.1037/a0022062

Egan, S.J., Wade, T.D., Shafran, R., & Antony, M.M. (2014). *Cognitive-behavioral treatment of perfectionism.* Guilford Press.

Epstein, L., & Mardon, S. (2007). *The Harvard Medical School guide to a good night's sleep.* McGraw-Hill.

Hasson, G. (2014). *Emotional intelligence. Managing emotions to make a positive impact on your life and career. Capstone.*

Parker, G., Tavella, G., & Eyers, K. (2021). *Burnout: A guide to identifying burnout and pathways to recovery.* Allen & Unwin.

Schwartz, T., & McCarthy, C. (2007). Manage your energy, not your time. *Harvard Business Review, Oct 2007.* https://hbr.org/2007/10/manage-your-energy-not-your-time

4. Outcomes

Clear, J. (2018). *Atomic habits. An easy & proven way to build good habits & break bad ones.* Random House.

Covey, S. (2004). *The 7 habits of highly effective people. Pocket Books.*

Dweck, C. S. (2017). *Mindset: The new psychology of success.* Robinson.

Parker, G., Tavella, G., & Eyers, K. (2021). *Burnout: A guide to identifying burnout and pathways to recovery.* Allen & Unwin.

5. Behaviour change

Clear, J. (2018). *Atomic habits. An easy & proven way to build good habits & break bad ones.* Random House.

Dweck, C. S. (2017). *Mindset: The new psychology of success.* Robinson.

Kwasnicka, D., Dombrowski, S.U., White, M., & Sniehotta, F. (2016). Theoretical explanations for maintenance of behaviour change: A systematic review of behaviour theories. *Health Psychology Review, 10*(3), 277-296. https://doi.org/10.1080/17437199.2016.1151372.

THE SKILL COLLECTIVE

We help individuals and organisations build skills for better wellbeing, mental health, and performance.

TheSkillCollective.com

www.ingramcontent.com/pod-product-compliance
Lightning Source LLC
Chambersburg PA
CBHW040743020526
44107CB00084B/2874